CRIMINALITY

INSIDE THE MINDS
OF CRIMINALS AND VICTIMS

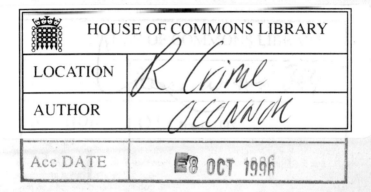
ART O'CONNOR

This book is dedicated to
Oonagh, Claire, Brian and Nóra

Acknowledgements

I would like to thank James Conway, Leo Mangan, Jo O'Donoghue and Anne O'Donnell.

First published in 1996 by
Marino Books
An imprint of Mercier Press
16 Hume Street Dublin 2

Trade enquiries to Mercier Press
PO Box 5, 5 French Church Street,
Cork

© Art O'Connor 1996

ISBN 1 86023 045 8

10 9 8 7 6 5 4 3 2 1

A CIP record for this title is available
from the British Library

Cover image courtesy of Midas
Productions
Cover design by Bluett
Set by Richard Parfrey
Printed in Ireland by ColourBooks,
Baldoyle Industrial Estate, Dublin 13

CONTENTS

INTRODUCTION

Why write a book about crime, criminals, victims and associated psychiatric issues? Crime seems to have a way of gripping the public imagination and although people are outraged and horrified by crime and criminals, they are also fascinated by them. Some of the most successful modern writers – including women like P. D. James and Patricia Cornwell – write about violent crime in a very explicit way. Crime is just as popular on television and in the cinema as in book form, no less so when it is based on fact, such as in documentary or news programmes, than when it is fiction.

Television police and crime series, too numerous to mention, have always been among the most popular programmes. For instance *Cracker*, a recent ITV series, has a police psychologist as hero. This marrying of crime and psychology is a winning combination. People have always been interested in what makes the murderer commit his crimes and in what makes other criminals tick.

When members of the public follow real-life criminal investigations in the media or real trials they often ask themselves about the mentality of the perpetrator of horrific crimes. From time to time they hear accounts of psychiatrists giving opinions about a defendant's mental state or they may hear discussions about insanity and diminished responsibility. People do not have a clear understanding of the input of psychiatrists in the whole process, yet there is a commonly held view that criminals often have psychiatric problems.

As a practising forensic psychiatrist I set out to provide for the interested reader an account of the association between psychiatry and crime, the region in which I spend my working life. I hope to share some of the issues, cases and topics I have found so fascinating during my career. The case material is made up of composite case histories which are based on many different cases, and I have added some fictional components to disguise identities.

Art O'Connor
Dublin
February 1996

PART I

Inside the Minds of Criminals

I
Murderers and Homicides

'I have Killed the Only Woman I ever Loved'
Murder is the intentional killing of another; manslaughter
is unintentional killing. Homicide is the general term for
this crime; special terms include patricide for the killing
of one's father and infanticide for the killing of an infant
by a mother. Homicide has long been accepted as the most
heinous of crimes and as a result murder still carries the
death penalty in many jurisdictions around the world. It
is one of the most feared crimes but also one of the most
fascinating. In the media a 'good murder' tops the news
coverage if it is available for reporting because journalists
know that people will read such a story or listen to it or
watch it on TV.

Jamie was twenty-five and married to Josie, aged twenty.
They had two children aged one and two. They lived in a
small flat in a large city. Jamie had no support from his
family and Josie's relationship with her parents had always
been stormy. She was still close to a single sister who lived
quite near. Her parents considered her to be wild and
stubborn. She had considered them to be extremely
restrictive towards her and was very glad when Jamie

initially suggested they move in together because she felt she would at last be independent.

Jamie loved Josie and was very attentive to her. They both loved the children but Josie sometimes found them a burden. She envied some of her school friends, with whom she still went out, because they were single and free. Although she liked her position as a grown-up person with children, she felt stifled. Jamie's attentions were all very well but she sometimes felt a little claustrophobic, like a bird in a cage. More and more Jamie questioned why she wanted to go out so much with her friends. What was wrong with staying home with him?

Jamie had always drunk a little more than he should and his drinking started to get worse. More and more he argued with Josie about the amount of time she spent outside their home with her friends. She got a part-time job in a bar and this upset him further. Jamie's drinking deteriorated and on several occasions he slapped Josie during their increasingly frequent arguments. This made him feel guilty as he had never been violent before. It made her feel a little frightened because he was a strong man and she was quite petite. She feared that he might become seriously violent at some point but she put the idea out of her mind.

Josie continued to go out with her friends and to work in the pub. Some nights she stayed with her sister, along with her children. They all enjoyed this new freedom and Josie sometimes wondered why she had needed to move in with Jamie to get away from her parents in the first place. She could cope with the children but now she found herself also having to cope with an increasingly difficult husband. He was often drunk and argumentative and she dreaded returning home to the inevitable rows and questions, which depressed her and sometimes frightened the children. Her situation was becoming worse than she could remember things being at home.

Josie decided to stay a few days with her sister to sort herself out and think about the future. She had never seriously thought she would be in this position about her relationship but she was confused. Her sister had suggested that she, Josie and the children set up house together and Josie was seriously thinking about this. The sister accepted her and the two children with no fuss and the children were happy in the new location.

In the flat Jamie was feeling sorry for himself. Josie had been away for two nights now and she had not got in touch with him. When she left she said she wanted a few days to sort herself out and think about things. He started to fear that he might be losing her and the children. He blamed her friends and her sister for having a bad influence on her. His drinking, already a serious problem, got even worse, and during the days Josie was away, he drank continuously.

On the third night Jamie was very drunk indeed. He had got through around twenty cans of lager during the day and during the course of the evening he consumed nearly a bottle of whiskey. In this intoxicated state he decided he was going to sort out his relationship with Josie once and for all. He thought he would frighten her with a knife so he put a sharp kitchen knife into his back pocket. If things did not work out he decided he would commit suicide rather than leave Josie behind. He put on his coat and went out into the rain. It was midnight.

The journey to Josie's sister's house took only about ten minutes. As Jamie walked he became more angry at Josie, her friends and her sister. He felt abandoned and helpless. He rang the doorbell and Josie's sister opened the door. She was shocked by his appearance – dripping wet and obviously angry and drunk. She tried to talk to him but he brushed past her and went into the living room where Josie was sitting. She too was shocked and frightened by how he looked. Her sister persuaded him to sit down. He sat but his angry state did not change. He was swearing and muttering and then he demanded that Josie and the children come home with him.

Josie had been very quiet but she now decided to stand her ground. Unfortunately, she underestimated how disturbed Jamie's state of mind was and how drunk he was. She went over to try to calm him, saying that she was not ready to return home. Jamie lunged at her with the knife and stabbed her once in the heart. The action was over in an instant. Blood gushed from Josie's chest and she walked backwards for a few steps. She sank slowly into a chair before losing consciousness.

Her sister was stunned – she and Josie had also been drinking for most of the evening – and it took her a few moments to respond. She was terrified of the drunken man who had just stabbed her sister. She managed to telephone for an ambulance and Josie was rushed to hospital. The ambulance men informed the police, who soon arrrived on the scene. A short time later, without regaining consciousness, Josie died in hospital from the heart wound. Jamie was arrested and subsequently found guilty of murder. It was claimed that he had intended to kill Josie and had carried the knife with him for that purpose. At the trial he said, 'I have killed the only woman I ever loved.'

The vast majority of homicide perpetrators are men and among the commonest victims are their wives or common-law partners. Girlfriends are also common victims, as are children. Sometimes one man might kill another in a row or fight, especially near to closing time in a pub. Sometimes rows develop on the night or some old argument rekindles itself because both men are drunk. The row comes to a fatal conclusion because one of them has a knife and draws it out to frighten the other man. The injuries may be multiple but it is common for a person to die from a single stab wound where the knife severs a vital artery or enters the heart, as in Josie's case. Frequently the assailant is found guilty of manslaughter and given a sentence of between five and ten years. If there is more that one stab wound the jury may be convinced that the killing was intentional so the person is found guilty of murder. Some violent and aggressive individuals are veterans of bar room fracas involving knives. They may have scars which they wear with pride. Alcohol is a very frequent factor in these situations and both parties in such altercations tend to have criminal histories and alcohol problems.

Homicide offenders are usually between twenty-five and thirty-five. Property offenders, such as burglars, tend to be in their late teens or early twenties, rapists in their mid twenties. In the great majority of homicides assailants and victims know each other. In over 30 per cent of cases they know each other very well; they are in fact spouses or other close relatives. In rape cases assailants and victims are known to each other in about 30 per cent of cases but they know each other only rarely in property offences.

CRIMES OF PASSION

It is not surprising that one of the commonest homicide situations is when a husband kills his wife. The relationship between a husband and wife or between other sexual partners is one of the most intense possible. Love and affection may give way to or even coexist with frustration and hatred. Spouses tend to blame each other, often quite unjustly. Husbands who work outside the home frequently return to vent the irritations and problems of the day on their wives and children, knowing that nobody outside the home would stand for this treatment. Such venting of the man's frustrations may lead to violence. If this is coupled with abuse of alcohol, the situation may be unpredictable, even dangerous.

Here is a typical situation where a wife is killed by her husband or partner. The couple may have been happy early on in the relationship but they no longer love each other very much. The man may be aggressive by nature and may have got into rows and fights over the years, especially when drinking to excess. There may already have been a small degree of violence in the relationship in the early years but this would have settled down. The children are approaching their teens and they stay out of the house as much as possible because of the father's moods. He always drank heavily but as he approaches his mid forties the drinking gets worse. There are signs that the company he works for may be closing down so he starts to drink more. The violence at home increases; he starts to beat his wife on a regular basis. He blames her if the house is not to his taste or if anything at all goes wrong. One night when he returns from the pub, very drunk, he has another row with her. He starts with blows and kicks but completely loses control and ends up strangling her. The terrified children upstairs hear the noise but are paralysed with fear.

Then there is quiet. After about ten minutes the eldest boy creeps downstairs. He finds his father sitting in a chair almost asleep. His mother is lying lifeless on the floor. The petrified child manages to phone the ambulance. The mother is dead on arrival at the hospital. The father is arrested later that night and charged with murder. His memory of what happened is patchy because of the effects of the alcohol (like many who abuse alcohol, he has a history of memory blackouts). He is eventually found guilty of murder and sentenced to life imprisonment.

The dangerous factors here are a history of increasing violence and wife-beating which is exacerbated by alcoholism. Excessive drinking makes people much more likely to lose control of their actions and their judgement. In a proportion of cases alcohol abuse also affects the memory. This is called an alcoholic memory blackout and is common in the person who has a history of alcohol abuse. Amnesia is no defence, of course, and neither is intoxication.

Jealousy
Jealousy is another reason why individuals (usually men)

kill their spouses or partners. Such abnormal jealousy totally dominates the lives of the people involved. This jealousy may be present from the beginning of the relationship but may get worse as the years go by. In such cases it is usually regarded as being part of the man's personality make-up. Sometimes, more rarely, jealousy develops for the first time at a later stage in the relationship and may be part of a mental illness such as schizophrenia. The man may have various delusions, one of them focusing on his wife's fidelity.

Excessive jealousy which comes to dominate a relationship is usually referred to as morbid jealousy syndrome, or, less commonly, as paranoid jealousy or the Othello syndrome. (In Shakespeare's *Othello* the hero kills his beloved wife, Desdemona, convinced that she is unfaithful by a clever scheme hatched by his lieutenant, Iago.) The man believes his wife is unfaithful. One individual may believe she is unfaithful with one other man, while another may believe that she is unfaithful with many partners. This is nearly always untrue but even when the man is faced with incontrovertible evidence that he is wrong, he sticks by his belief. The morbid extent of the jealousy may only become fully evident after the marriage and sometimes only after several years. The man may frequently argue with the woman and accuse her of having affairs or relationships. He may question her minutely and endlessly about her movements and whereabouts during every period of the day, causing her great distress.

(Occasionally, very rarely, one comes across cases where the morbidly jealous person is a wife. Some morbidly jealous women are capable of violence, as men

are, but the violence does not seem to become as dangerous as in the case of men.)

The jealous man may follow his wife everywhere and
even hire a detective to find proof of her infidelities. Even
though this is almost never forthcoming his conviction
that he is right remains as strong as ever. He may start
checking the woman's underwear for signs of sexual
activity such as hairs or semen. He may insist on physically searching and examining the woman. He may monitor
all her telephone calls and even insist that she stay at
home most of the time. She may be allowed out only when
he is with her. In such situations he may become very
angry if she speaks to another man even in a shop. He
may accuse her of being attracted to other men she sees
on the street or even on television.

The most serious problem with such morbidly jealous
men is that they are capable of violence. This may be
manifested through wife battering in a constant pattern
or in response to real or imagined contact with men. If
the woman does not give the correct answers to her
partner's unremitting questions he may respond in a
violent way. Sometimes the violence is for no special
reason other than that the man feels like it. Life becomes
hell for the woman.

The violence may be pushing, punching, kicking, head-
butting or anything else that one can imagine. In the early
phase of the problem the injuries may be only in areas
that will not be seen by the outside world such as the body
or the upper arms and legs. All types of abuse are possible,
including burns and attempted strangling. In some cases the
perpetrator kills the woman and is charged with murder.

Alcohol has an interesting part to play in these cases. Between 10 and 20 per cent of men who have the morbid jealousy syndrome also have a serious alcohol problem. The partner of a man who comes home very drunk at night may be unwilling to have sex with him, enough to convince the morbidly jealous man that she is having an affair with someone else. An intoxicated man may have difficulties achieving and sustaining an erection and this he may also blame on his wife. A drunk and angry jealous man is particularly dangerous if he has harboured violent intentions against his wife or her supposed lovers. When he is sober he may be able to contain such impulses but not when he is drunk.

So many individuals of the paranoid or morbidly jealous group have alcohol problems that one could postulate that there is a causal connection of some kind. Does the alcohol cause some subtle form of brain damage that results in this syndrome? We just do not know if this is the case or not. We do know, however, that many men with the syndrome are dry alcoholics, which means that continuous drinking is not required for the problem to arise or persist. Again, many of these men have no alcohol problem at all.

Erotomania, also called De Clerambault's syndrome, is comparable to the morbid jealousy or Othello syndrome. A flavour of this was seen in the well known film *Fatal Attraction*, where a woman becomes totally obsessed with a man and is determined to get him at all costs. The real-life situation has many similarities. The individual in question, whether male or female – the situation usually applies to heterosexuals – is not just in love but becomes disturbed by being totally absorbed in the object of his or her devotion.

In a typical scenario, there may have been some connection between the two individuals beforehand but frequently there is none at all. For instance, a junior clerk in a large company may become infatuated by the managing director. He may recognise her although he may never have actually met her. When he sees her in a corridor, every gesture she makes confirms to him that she loves him and that they are going to be married, that she is only waiting for the right time to announce it to the world. He may send her messages and little presents or flowers. These may be anonymous at first and puzzle the recipient. Later his identity will become clear: he may wait for her outside her office, in the foyer of the company building, eventually outside her home. As time goes on she may be inundated with love letters and other material in the post at work and at home. She may get repeated telephone calls from him and the whole situation can become very embarrassing, annoying and ultimately exhausting. The woman may initially have to explain to her husband and, as time goes on, to everyone else. The husband may also come in for a certain amount of pressure from the disturbed man. He is perceived as the person who is preventing the love object from marrying the rightful person. As a result he may be sent insulting and threatening letters and be subjected to unpleasant telephone calls. The couple and their family may suffer considerable distress.

Such disorders tend to be long-lasting and the situation can go on for years. The police find it difficult to act if the person does not commit a criminal offence such as an assault. The threatening messages in the post may sometimes be used to charge the person but they are regarded as minor offences. The besotted person may appear perfectly normal in other aspects of his or her life and lead an ordinary productive existence but in this one area he or she is highly abnormal and out of control.

Although a small number of such obsessives suffer from a mental illness such as schizophrenia, the majority are not mentally ill in the ordinary sense and will not comply with medication or a trial of any treatment. Many do not respond in any case and hardly any believe they have a problem. If their behaviour is threatening the courts can sometimes help with injunctions and barring orders but these are of limited use.

Famous people – Madonna and Princess Anne come to mind – may be haunted by such obsessive individuals and come to fear for their safety. John Lennon was killed by a stalker. There is no easy solution for the victims and their lives and the lives of their families can be seriously affected. Threats, money, persuasion and the law all seem to be ineffective; nobody really understands why such people persist in this kind of behaviour.

After a time, the infatuated, apparently love-sick person may change into an angry unrequited lover who resents and then hates the previously loved person. He or she may have violent feelings towards the person for not acknowledging them and returning their love or may develop a morbid jealousy syndrome. The person most at risk when this happens is the love object. When violence comes into the picture the criminal justice system has a little more to offer in terms of protection from the police and the courts. It is a pity that things have to go so far – sometimes as far as serious injury or murder – before the individual can be protected.

HOMICIDE OF CHILDREN

Children are usually victims of homicide in the context of child battering. This is mostly a male offence and it may involve wife battering as well. The offender, usually in his twenties, may be an egocentric and immature man who is demanding of his wife as a child might be. He may even be jealous of the time and attention the child gets from the mother. The wife battering may have a similar childish basis as the man takes his episodic feelings of anger and frustration out on the unfortunate woman. The man may become violent towards the child because he says he or she is crying too much. Such children sometimes do cry a lot because they are not getting enough care and attention and sometimes because they may have minor injuries to various parts of their bodies. Physical abuse of children is rarely a once-off event and when such a child is finally killed there is usually a history of previous abuse.

The child may be the man's own but often he or she is a stepchild. Part of the man's jealous feelings may be related to his partner's previous relationship, of which the child is a visible reminder. Sometimes the abused child is fostered or adopted by the couple. The abuse of the mother may occur during a pregnancy and the abuse of both mother and child may continue after the child is born.

Methods of killing a child are as numerous as the ways

in which a child can be abused. Hitting, punching, hitting with objects, scalding, burning, anything that one's imagination can dream up – all have been seen. A common phenomenon in recent years is 'the shaking baby syndrome', where the child is taken up by the man and shaken until he or she stops crying or goes unconscious. This is a very violent form of assault, resulting in repeated whiplash injuries to the neck combined with repeated injuries to the infant's brain inside the skull. The child may be left paralysed or mentally handicapped if he or she survives and clearly some do not survive. Some offenders hold objects over a child's mouth until they lose consciousness and others strangle the child.

Some child abusers and murderers are not immature young men who are jealous of their child but violent and bullying men who may have a history of violent offending of various kinds. Their history may be complicated by alcohol or drug abuse and violence is a way of life for them. They are often angry individuals who are quick to lose their tempers. Sadly, they do not confine their outbursts to adults who may be able to defend themselves and their children are sometimes targets.

Fathers are not the only perpetrators. Sometimes mothers kill their children too, although much less frequently. Bernie was an unmarried mother in her early twenties She and her six-month-old son lived at home with her parents, with whom she did not have a good relationship. The relationship with the father of her son had ended during the pregnancy and he never came to see her or his child. She was often unhappy with her life and spent most of her time with her child in her small room. Bernie had no contact with former friends; from early on in her life she had had a difficult personality and did not get on very well at school. Alcohol became a problem for her in her late teens and so did sedative medication. When she felt low, as often happened, her future seemed bleak to her.

One evening she was feeling particularly unhappy and alone. She and the infant were the only ones in the house still awake. The child was unwell and cried a lot. The more the child cried the worse Bernie felt. Suicide had crossed her mind from time to time in recent months but she had never gone as far as making suicide plans. On this evening Bernie took several sleeping tablets and some whiskey because she had been having difficulties sleeping over the previous week. She held the crying child tightly in her arms, then held a cushion over his mouth until the crying stopped. She continued to hold the cushion there until the child stopped breathing, then she put him in his cot and went to sleep.

This is a very sad and shocking story. The child was dead and everyone involved, including the grandparents, was severely traumatised. Bernie was found guilty of infanticide, which is legally comparable to manslaughter. It is a defence that is available to the small number of women who kill their infant child of less than twelve months, in the context of a serious mental disorder. Bernie spent six months in a psychiatric hospital but there was never any clear evidence of mental illness such as schizophrenia or depression. She had an unusual personality disorder but this does not explain why she killed the child. Bernie herself will probably never fully understand why she did it. It was accepted by the court that she was in extreme emotional turmoil after the pregnancy and that this constituted a depressive disorder. Professionals sometimes have to admit to being baffled by cases such as these. One can postulate that mothers such as Bernie were intending to commit suicide but did not go the whole way. Perhaps it was an angry gesture against the people she knew or against society in general for not taking better care of her.

Infanticide is an offence that has been recognised for hundreds of years. From the beginning of the last century the thinking has been that the mind of a woman may have been unbalanced by the effects of childbirth or lactation. If this were established in court the woman would be treated as humanely as possible. Sometimes this meant a short stay in prison; more usually a short period in a psychiatric hospital. If there were a conviction it was legally the same as manslaughter, which means that the judge could deal with sentencing as he or she saw fit. Most people would agree that this is appropriate because the perpetrators of infanticide are usually ill rather than criminal, suffering from severe postnatal depression or from a puerperal psychosis [mental illness occurring in connection with childbirth] which can be similar to schizophrenia.

We still see cases of infanticide from time to time but they are normally no longer dealt with by the criminal justice system or the courts. The perpetrators are given treatment rather than punishment. When these women recover from their illness it is difficult for them to come to terms with what they have done. If a woman who has committed infanticide has another child, it is vital that she and the new child are carefully monitored by doctors and social workers for several years lest the mental disturbance should recur. With serious postnatal psychiatric disorders like postnatal depression or psychosis the chance of recurrence in subsequent pregnancies is about 20 per cent. A small number of psychiatric hospitals have special mother and infant units to monitor such situations or fresh cases of postnatal psychiatric problems. These aim to treat the mother and protect the child by monitoring their interaction on a twenty-four-hour basis.

Not all children who are killed by their mothers are tiny infants. Some are older so the defence of infanticide does not apply. Julie was in her late twenties and in an unhappy marriage. She and her husband had two daughters, aged three and four. Her parents and family lived in a different country so she was dependent on her husband for everything. Julie was intelligent but she had made no friends since moving to the new country. She had no formal psychiatric history but she felt depressed from time to time. On one occasion she took an overdose of sleeping tablets but she slept it off over twenty-four hours and did not seek any help at that time. By now her marriage was in difficulties and she was anxious for her own future and that of her children.

She had already started drinking in the evenings and sometimes took two or three sleeping tablets rather than the one per night reluctantly prescribed by the family doctor. Nothing seemed to make any difference for her; she felt there was nowhere to turn and no one to help.

Finally her husband and she decided to separate. One day Julie was sitting by herself at home in the kitchen. She saw a child's skipping rope on a table. She picked it up and walked outside. Her younger child and a neighbour's child were playing at the back of the houses. Julie called them over and strangled both of them with the rope.

Julie was arrested soon afterwards. Despite many investigations and examinations no evidence of mental illness was found. She was found guilty of murder and sentenced to life imprisonment. One can only speculate as to why she committed the offence. Was it in some bizarre way a cry for help by a desperate woman to society and to her husband? Or was it an act of defiance and anger because of the breakdown of her marriage?

An interesting case of child murder occurred in Ireland in the last century. An unfortunate widow, who had three children, became mentally ill. The children were aged one, two and three. The distraught woman believed that her dead husband was communicating with her and she was looking forward to being reunited with him again. He told her that she must kill the children and herself in order that they could join him in heaven. She resolved to kill the three children and herself with boiling water. She boiled a large quantity of water, put it into a bath and scalded the three children to death. She then put her own head into the boiling water but was later found by neighbours and taken to hospital. According to newspaper reports she sustained hideous scarring. At the conclusion of her trial she was found not guilty by reason of insanity and spent many years in a special security psychiatric institution.

There must be some category of person that is totally safe for children, someone who is never seen in the context of child killing. Surely children are safe from their grand-mothers? Even here there is the odd exception. A woman in her mid seventies, a widow, had two grown up children, a boy and a girl. Both her children were married and lived several miles away from her. Her daughter had two little boys aged one and two and the elderly woman loved them very much. From time to time her daughter asked her to babysit for her when she and her husband were going out. For several weeks the old woman had seemed a little more argumentative than usual but the daughter and other people who knew her paid no attention. One weekend the old woman babysat as usual for the daughter. When the daughter returned home in the early hours of the morning she found her mother sitting in a chair crying. She had strangled the two small children.

Later she revealed that she had started to believe in a different type of god from the God of her traditional religious upbringing. She believed that God had told her he was coming to Earth and that it was near the end of the world. He ordered her to kill the children so that they would be saved. She believed this so she killed the two grandchildren. At her trial she was found to be guilty but insane. She had started to suffer from late-onset schizo-phrenia and she experienced auditory hallucinations and delusions about God. The trial judge committed her to a security psychiatric institution.

Cases of this kind are extremely rare.

PATRICIDE

The killing of one's father is not a common offence and when it occurs it makes headlines. One sometimes comes across cases where a father and his sons get into a drunken brawl after a day of drinking and during the fight one of the men is killed. The father is just as likely to be the dead one as any of the others. In the US a recent spectacular case involved two young men killing both of their parents. They apparently had been given a very privileged and sumptuous upbringing by the wealthy parents. After the killings they talked about ill treatment and abuse as a justification for their actions.

Another situation that is seen from time to time is an abusing father being killed by a teenage son. The man may have battered his wife over a period and may also have sexually abused his children. If the offender is able to convince the court that he was justified in acting as he did he is found not guilty of murder but of manslaughter on the basis of provocation. The courts in general deal leniently with these cases.

Patricide is the basis of the plot of the Greek tragedy by Sophocles, *Oedipus Rex*, in which the hero unknowingly kills his father Laius and marries his mother, Jocasta. At the turn of the century Sigmund Freud used the Oedipus myth to develop a theory which became known as the 'Oedipus complex'. This he defined as the unconscious desire of the male child to kill his father, replace him as the head of the family and marry his mother. Though this theory has many detractors, it has been very influential in modern psychology as well as in modern literature and art.

An individual who kills his or her father is usually mentally ill. The cases are sad and disturbing because they leave a long legacy of trauma and guilt in the family and social network. One such case involved a young woman in the UK who had suffered from schizophrenia since her mid teens. At the time in question she was in her early thirties. Her parents were about seventy years of age and not very well physically. The other children of the family were grown up and married. The daughter with schizophrenia was single and still lived in the family home. She had made her parents' lives a misery over the years because of her demands and accusations about conspiracies. She sometimes heard hallucinatory voices and she would shout back at them because they were often insulting to her. This shouting often occurred at night and caused a lot of disruption in the house and sleepless nights for her parents. They wanted only what was best for her and consequently they needed to have her committed to the local psychiatric hospital on several occasions over the years. She resented this and never forgave them.

One of the delusions from which this woman suffered was that people were trying to harm her. She was convinced that her father was part of the conspiracy and she decided to kill him. One night, as he dozed in front of the television, she strangled him from behind. He was dead on admission to hospital. She was committed to hospital and subsequently charged with murder. At the trial she was found guilty of manslaughter on the grounds of diminished responsibility, a defence available only in the UK, and she was committed to a maximum security psychiatric institution.

Another case involved a man, also in his thirties, who had a long history of what is known as a schizoaffective disorder. This is similar to schizophrenia: sufferers have episodes of illness where they experience unpleasant persecutory delusions or disturbing auditory hallucinations. Coupled with this they often have significant mood disorders, most commonly depression but sometimes mania. During a relapse in his mental illness this young man had a delusion that his father was an evil leader of a gang of criminals in the city where they lived, a delusion which had also been prominent in previous episodes of his illness. He believed that his father was involved in murders and drug pushing. He also believed he was the central figure in a child sexual abuse network. This was all untrue and totally a product of the son's mental illness; the father had never had any involvement in crime.

One evening the man decided to kill his father. He had given vague hints of this intentions over the years but people around him felt there was no chance that he would carry it out. On the night in question he killed his father with a kitchen knife as the father lay asleep in bed. The terrified mother woke up to find the dreadful scene in her bedroom. Her dead husband was lying beside her, her son holding the bloody knife. As in the previous case, the offender was found guilty of manslaughter on the grounds of diminished responsibility. He too was committed to a special security hospital for treatment.

MATRICIDE
Matricide, the killing of a woman by one of her children, is even rarer than patricide and the offender is nearly

always seriously mentally disturbed. A mother is usually regarded as the most important source of nurturing, protection and comfort in the whole of human life and seems thus the least likely person to be killed by her own child – under normal circumstances. Sadly, some mothers are not very loving or caring and sometimes a particular set of circumstances may produce a very abnormal situation. The following two cases illustrate unusual domestic dramas that ended in matricide.

Sharon was forty years of age and mentally handicapped. She lived alone with her elderly mother in a rural area in the UK. Her father had died five years previously. There was one older brother who was married and lived in the nearest town, which was ten miles away. He rarely visited them. The two women had had a rather strained relationship since the father's death. Sharon had been much closer to her father than her mother and she found it very difficult to cope with his death. She was liable to be demanding and wilful like a difficult and stubborn child and although she loved her father a lot she was also a little afraid of him. He had therefore been able to keep her behaviour in check.

After her father's death, Sharon started staying out late whenever she felt like it and refused to clean her room or help in the house. She stopped looking after herself and her mother frequently had to argue to get her to bathe or to do anything at all constructive. From time to time Sharon drank whiskey which she bought in the local supermarket and when she was drunk her behaviour was even worse. She scolded her mother for nagging her and sometimes slapped her. It was a terrible situation for the frail elderly woman.

One evening Sharon and her mother had an argument after Sharon had been drinking. It was late and the old woman was preparing to go to bed. She had told Sharon to stop drinking and her daughter responded with the usual tirade of abuse. But tonight Sharon's mood was different. Her angry feelings did not settle down. She had often thought that life would be better without her mother and hoped that she would die. As the mother walked up the stairs the argument continued and Sharon became violently angry. She followed the old woman and knocked her down the stairs. The mother had a very bad fall to the bottom and was nearly unconscious. Sharon, still furious, went back down the stairs. She kicked and punched her mother as she lay on the ground and stopped only when she saw that she was dead.

At that stage Sharon panicked and ran half a mile down the road to a neighbour's house. The neighbour could not make sense of what she was saying so she accompanied her back to her home. They found the mother covered in blood at the bottom of the stairs. Sharon insisted that her mother had fallen down the stairs. The ambulance was called but the old woman was dead before she arrived at the hospital. The medical staff informed the police, who arrested Sharon the next morning. She continued to insist that the old woman had fallen down the stairs, despite the huge amount of forensic and medical evidence supporting the view that she had killed her. Very close to her trial she agreed to a plea of manslaughter on the grounds of diminished responsibility. This was accepted by the court because of her low intelligence and she was committed to a centre for the mentally handicapped.

Jake was in his mid forties. He lived with his widowed mother who suffered from serious arthritis and was wheelchair bound. She was in her late seventies. Jake was the youngest of four boys and he had been tacitly marked out by the others as the one who would stay at home to mind the ageing parents. The father had died from dementia three years earlier. Jake had nursed his father through the difficult years of decline and even tried to care for him at home when he became incontinent. This had put an enormous strain on Jake, which contributed to his developing an alcohol problem. He used alcohol initially because he was not able to sleep but then he became dependent on it. His mother was becoming an invalid at the same time so that even when his father died Jake's burden was not lifted.

Jake's mother had been a domineering woman in the household throughout his life, and she continued to treat him like a child. If he stayed out late or returned home intoxicated she never missed an opportunity to berate him and complain. They had constant arguments and Jake found it increasingly difficult to cope with the situation. She frequently ridiculed him for not being a proper man and getting married like his brothers, although they both knew that she could not cope alone.

One night he returned home very late and very drunk. His mood had been down for several weeks but he had not sought help from his family doctor or the rest of the family. The future seemed very black to him and he thought of suicide. He hoped for his mother's death as the only way out. Perhaps he would kill her and then himself. When he arrived home he sat in the kitchen in this miserable and hopeless state. His mother was asleep but when she realised he was in, she shouted something about his being drunk again. This was the last straw. Jake lost control. He went upstairs and into the mother's room. He quickly took one of the pillows and held it over her face until she stopped breathing. There was very little struggle. When it was over he broke down and cried for a long time. Then he called the ambulance and the police.

At his trial it was accepted he had been under persistent and unusual pressure for a long time. It was also accepted that his action was on the spur of the moment, against a background of great unhappiness and distress. He was found guilty of manslaughter and given a short custodial sentence. On his release from prison Jake was able to get help with his alcohol problem. The family sold the family home and divided the proceeds. Jake moved to a different area. Although the rest of the family still see him, they have never really forgiven him for killing their mother.

FRATRICIDE AND SORORICIDE

Siblings may sometimes feel like killing each other while they are growing up but this feeling seldom becomes a reality. Some brothers and sisters have a very pleasant and close relationship which persists into adulthood, while other sets of siblings seem to be forever arguing and fighting. This kind of relationship may also persist into adulthood.

From time to time one comes across strange cases

where childhood tussles and fights have taken on a different intensity. One such case involved a teenage boy who had a bad relationship with his two-year-old sister. He was jealous of the younger child because she was bright and attractive and seemed to get more attention from his parents, as well as from other relatives and friends. When he was left to babysit his sister he would sometimes hit her or lock her in a dark room.

One night the child was unwell and cried a lot. The older boy was very irritated by this and he hit her to make her stop crying. This did not work so he strangled her. The teenager was eventually brought to court and found guilty of manslaughter. He was given a prison sentence of five years. There was no evidence of mental illness but the boy had a strange personality makeup which allowed the common childhood fantasy of killing someone you do not like become reality. He never showed much remorse for what he did.

The biblical story of Cain murdering Abel is the archetypal murder of a man by his brother. In real life one brother will most commonly kill another when there is a fight of some kind. Alcohol is frequently part of this picture. Two brothers, both in their early twenties, had had unhappy early lives. Their father was an alcoholic and he often beat them and their mother. The main thing that united them was their hatred of their father. They both lived away from home.

The two brothers were heavy drinkers and when they met at the weekends they usually became very drunk together. When drunk they often had arguments, even fights. Their worst injuries would be a black eye and they would be friends again the following day. Indeed, the amount they had drunk often made them have a very hazy memory of the events of the previous evening. One evening after a night's drinking they had a fight near the pub. During the row, which was about a card game earlier in the evening, one brother knocked the other to the ground. As he fell he hit his head on a rock and lost consciousness. The other brother continued to hit him until he realised he was not moving. Then he panicked and ran back into the pub to phone an ambulance. The man died from brain damage in hospital several days later.

The surviving brother had a very hazy memory of what happened. He remembered the staring eyes of the dead brother and this image returned for many months in his dreams. He was arrested later on the evening of the fight. Subsequently he was found guilty of manslaughter and given a short custodial sentence.

The killing of a sister by a brother is quite rare. The perpetrator of such an offence may be mentally ill and believe that the sister is part of some conspiracy to harm him. Another unusual case is where the sister is suffering from a mental disorder such as schizophrenia or mental handicap and the perpetrator is sane. June was a woman in her late twenties who suffered from mental handicap. She lived at home with her brother and her elderly parents. Her brother, David, was five years older than her. The older siblings were living away from home and seldom visited because of June's behaviour. This had caused her parents much distress and unhappiness since the onset of the behavioural problems in her teens.

For several years June had been very demanding and argumentative. She wanted meals in her room and frequently banged the floor for attention. At night she insisted on looking at television with the volume turned up full. About once a year her behaviour became so intolerable that she needed to be committed to the local psychiatric hospital. Her parents hated these times because they felt guilty. However, there was a silent sigh of relief from the whole family because they could then have a brief glimpse of normality.

David felt completely tied by the domestic situation. He was the only healthy one living in the house. He looked after the two ageing parents whom he loved and he also had to care for the mentally handicapped sister whom he had grown to hate. He had the helpless feeling that his life was passing him by. David was not a good mixer and had always been introverted. As the years went on he felt increasingly isolated. There were no opportunities for him to meet people in his job. It was many years since he had had a girlfriend. David saw as his main tormentor the sister who dominated the whole household. He started to drink heavily on a regular basis, at first buying some beer on the way home from work. The drink problem escalated and most nights he got drunk at home while looking at the television as he tried to ignore the noise from June's room.

One evening David got particularly drunk. He sat up until three in the morning and was both intoxicated and exhausted. June's shouting and banging had stopped only half an hour earlier. Crying to himself, David decided he could not continue in this living hell. When he turned off the television he made a decision through a haze of alcohol. He went into his sister's room and he looked at her for a minute as she slept. Her light and radio were on as usual. Dave picked up a heavy metal ornament that was in the room, a statue of a dog, and hit June with it several times on the head. She made some groaning noises and he hit her some more. Then he cried and went into his parents' room and woke his father. He told him what he had done but for several minutes the older man could not make sense of what he was saying.

David and his father called an ambulance and later the police. June was dead. At the trial the whole sad story was told and the court expressed sympathy for all concerned. David was found guilty of manslaughter and given a five-year sentence. Half the sentence was suspended. The judge told David that he had sympathy for him but he had to insist on his spending some time in prison because he had killed another human being. While he was in prison, and later, he was given help for his alcohol problem and also for the depressive disorder that he had originally developed before he killed his sister. It took him a long time to come to terms with what he had done.

HOMICIDE OFFENDERS WITH MENTAL ILLNESS

It is thought that in about a third of homicide cases there is some psychiatric problem in the perpetrator. The commonest psychiatric illness associated with homicide is depression and the next commonest is schizophrenia. There is also an association with alcoholism and up to 60 per cent of perpetrators are intoxicated at the time of the killings. Anti-social personality disorder is also seeen in a proportion of these offenders. The man who killed his mentally handicapped sister suffered from both alcoholism and depression. The alcoholic person who commits homicide frequently does so in the context of a fight with another drunken person. These sad dramas may involve friends fighting over something trivial and then a knife is drawn. The survivor may not even properly remember the incident and he may be informed that he killed his friend only when he has sobered up in a police cell. Another common alcohol-influenced situation is the drunken wife-beater who goes too far and strangles or stabs his wife.

An interesting variant of the depressive homicide is the extended suicide. This is where a seriously depressed individual, usually a man, is so mentally ill that he experiences delusions, for instance that he is dying from some terrible disease and is going to suffer great pain and torment. He believes that all his loved ones will suffer the same ordeal. The mentally ill person decides that he must commit suicide to avoid all this and that he must kill his loved ones for the same reason. The decision to kill them is born out of love, not anger or hatred. One sometimes read about cases where a whole family is found dead, the wife and children shot in their beds, the man found dead in another room with his shotgun lying beside him. Such an individual will usually have a history of depression but people around him would never have suspected his potential for violence and suicide.

Our knowledge of these cases comes from the small number of surviving perpetrators who have failed to complete their extended suicide plan. They are usually found to be extremely depressed with delusions of diseases such as cancer or AIDS, and they may believe that they have been responsible for infecting the whole family. Others believe that a nuclear war is imminent and that the whole family will die horribly. Some may hear voices telling them that they must kill themselves and the family to save them and mankind from hell and damnation.

It is hard to understand why the vast majority of the perpetrators of extended suicides are men. It may be related to the fact that male suicides in general tend to be more violent than the female equivalent. Suicide by hanging, drowning, jumping off bridges or buildings are all more likely to be committed by the male, as are suicides by using weapons such as guns or knives.

After depression, schizophrenia is the most significant mental illness which is seen in association with homicide. There is usually a history of psychiatric illness and treatment over years and of symptoms of active mental illness at the time of the incident.

Kate, a woman living in the UK, had suffered from schizophrenia from her late teens. In her early years at secondary school she had performed very well academically and all agreed that she had great potential. But in her final year her performance deteriorated and she became very withdrawn. Her parents consulted the family doctor, who advised referral to the local psychiatric service. An initial diagnosis of depression was made but that was changed to schizophrenia after several months as strange behaviour emerged. Kate had started putting papers in her ears because she was hearing voices. The local services arranged for her admission to hospital, where she stayed for four months.

Kate was in now in her thirties. She lived in a council flat in a city centre area. From time to time she needed to be admitted to a psychiatric hospital for treatment when the schizophrenia went into relapse. This was usually precipitated by Kate deciding that she did not need to take her medication. At those times she stopped attending the day centre and her fortnightly psychiatric out-patient appointments. When she started to relapse her delusions became more intense, as did the auditory hallucinations that caused her so much suffering. She often had delusions about evil and the devil.

Kate woke up one morning, convinced that the devil was around her flat and inside her body. She could hear garbled voices talking about hell and saying that she had to die. These experiences continued throughout the day. She could not sit still so she walked continuously around the flat and the local streets, going in and out of shopping centres, shops and even churches. She could find no relief and became frightened that something terrible was going to happen to her and to other people.

One elderly man whom she knew saw that she was distressed and invited her in for a cup of tea. She had spoken to this man before and he was always kind to her. He knew that Kate lived in a group of flats owned by the local psychiatric service and he always tried to be friendly with the people who lived there. When the man went into the kitchen to make tea, Kate became convinced that this was all a trap and that the old man was part of the devil's army. She knew she must kill him to save herself and others as well. This she did by hitting him on the head from behind with a poker. Initially Kate was happy that she had killed a devil for the sake of all mankind but then she realised she had made a mistake. She ran away but was soon picked up by police. At her trial she was found to be of diminished responsibility and she was committed to a maximum security psychiatric facility.

Cases such as Kate's are very rare. In fact schizophrenics normally commit only minor offences, like stealing food from a shop in order to survive because they are unable to look after themselves properly. It is unfortunate that heavily reported crimes such as Kate's linger in the mind of the public and tend to make people frightened of mental illness.

DEFENCES TO CHARGES OF MURDER

The most satisfactory defence to a charge of murder or manslaughter is self defence. If you can prove that you were simply protecting yourself you will be acquitted of the charge and you can walk free. The jury must be satisfied that you believed you were in danger of being killed or seriously injured. If your assailant is about to slap you on the face and you kill him, with the intention of killing him or seriously injuring him, that is not self defence but murder.

The next defence is provocation. If you can prove that you acted as you did because the other person provoked you beyond a level that the ordinary man could endure the charge of murder will be reduced to manslaughter. The ordinary man is defined as the 'man at the top of the Clapham omnibus' and whether or not the provocation you endured is too much for the ordinary man will be decided by the jury. The provocation may consist of threats or insults directed at you or your family. The reaction to the provocation must be almost reflex and if there is any time lag, the jury may decide that your actions were premeditated and convict you of murder.

The most widely used psychiatric defence to murder in the UK is that of diminished responsibility. It is used only in murder cases and if it is successful it reduces the conviction from murder to manslaughter. If it can be shown at the trial that you were suffering from an 'abnormality of mind' at the time of the killing which 'substantially diminished' your mental responsibility for your actions, the conviction is reduced. The mandatory life sentence no longer applies and the judge may even decide to commit you to a psychiatric hospital for treatment. The abnormalities of mind usually allowed are the serious varieties of mental illness such as schizophrenia or depression, serious mental handicap and serious personality disorders. If the person is still suffering from a mental illness at the time of the trial, the judge usually commits him or her to a psychiatric hospital for treatment. He may arrange for something similar for the mentally handicapped person, depending on his needs and the available services. In the past, courts used to commit people with serious personality disorders, found guilty of manslaughter on the grounds of diminished responsibility, to high security hospitals. Such disorders are usually called 'psychopathic disorders'. In recent years courts are more likely to give such people prison sentences, including life imprisonment. In about 20 per cent of murder cases in the UK the defence of diminished responsibility is successfully used. About one-third of these offenders are sent to psychiatric hospitals, one-third are given life imprisonment and one-third get other disposals such as shorter sentences or probation.

The only psychiatric defence available in Irish law is the insanity defence. It can be used in any charge but it is normally used only in murder cases. The main part of the defence is what are known as the 'McNaughton Rules', after the case in 1843 that originated them. Daniel McNaughton tried to shoot the prime minister of England, Sir Robert Peel. He was suffering from paranoid schizo-phrenia and he believed that Sir Robert and the Tory party were persecuting him. He missed Sir Robert and instead shot his secretary, Edward Drummond. At trial he was found not guilty by reason of insanity and sent to a psychiatric hospital. This caused a public outcry and the Law Lords were asked to define the insanity rules for courts; hence the McNaughton Rules. These assume that the person is sane so if you raise the insanity defence you have to prove it. You must first show that at the time of the offence the offender suffered from a 'disease of the mind'. This usually means schizophrenia or serious depression. You must also prove that at that time the offender did not understand what he was doing or that what he was doing was wrong.

Since the 1970s an extra limb has been allowed: that the offender was unable to stop himself acting in the way he did because of the disease of the mind. This usually means that because of the delusions he was suffering from, he killed the other person in order to save his own life. It may have been that he thought the other person was really the devil, as in Kate's case, and that he was going to kill him and members of his family. In Ireland the defence of insanity is successful once a year or in approximately one out of twenty murder cases. When defendants are found guilty but insane they are committed to the only high security hospital in Ireland, the Central Mental Hospital. The length of stay is determined by the Department of Justice. The average stay is about ten years but many people stay longer.

MULTIPLE KILLERS

There are two main varieties of multiple killers. Serial killers kill a number of people over a period, often in a stereotyped way. Mass killers kill a large number of people at one time and often end their own lives in their final act of destruction. Serial killers have always fascinated people and fictional accounts of their exploits have been the basis of many successful crime and suspense writers' careers – think, for instance, of Hannibal Lecter in *Silence of the Lambs*. Real life serial killer stories are often more bizarre and incredible than fiction. For instance the murders of Fred and Rosemary West in Gloucester have been called the 'crimes of the century'. The aspects the public have found most astonishing are that a woman was involved, that the Wests abused, tortured and killed some of their own children and that neither of the Wests appear to have been suffering from any psychiatric disturbance.

In the case of Peter Sutcliffe, the Yorkshire Ripper, who killed thirteen women from 1975 to 1981, the serial killing was different. Sutcliffe was suffering from paranoid schizophrenia and he had a delusion that the voice of God told him to kill prostitutes, although not all his victims were prostitutes. At his trial in 1981 he was found guilty of thirteen murders despite the considerable medical that he was seriously mentally ill. Eventually, in 1984, Mr Sutcliffe was transferred to a high security psychiatric hospital for treatment.

Other famous serial killers include the Moors murderers of the 1960s and Dennis Nilsen who lived in Muswell Hill, London and was found guilty of six murders and two attempted murders in 1983 – again despite the efforts of his defence team to prove that he was suffering from a personality disorder.

It appears that many serial killers seem to want to be caught at some point. They either can no longer cope with what they are doing or they cannot keep it to themselves. They want to be famous and known as great killers. Very few such killers have a formal mental illness such a schizophrenia or manic depression. They frequently have strange antisocial personalities but are often quite intelligent. Nobody knows why they decide to take the lives of their victims. They usually target particular types of victims such as young blonde women, students, black male children or prostitutes, but some murder a variety of types of people. Some seek sex, sexual sadism and control over another human being. The sheer excitement and exhilaration of such total domination gives them the buzz they require. They seem not to value human life and to regard their victims as objects or playthings.

For some months or years they may have entertained fantasies of violence and in particular sexual violence. As time goes on they may make imaginary plans and even stake out victims without going any further. Eventually they pass over some dividing line and they decide to try out their fantasy for real. They may feel a mounting tension and excitement which they can hardly contain. They choose a victim and go through the procedure, which is well rehearsed in fantasy. It usually involves capturing a victim, sexually assault, torture and finally murder. When one killing is over the killer may feel that this is the end but the feelings all come back again and the process repeats itself. An added excitement may be evading and even humiliating the police. Some like the media attention that capture entails and even in custody they may avidly read about themselves in the newspapers and watch news items about their case on television.

Mass killers tend also not to be mentally ill, although they may have a history of being odd and introverted. Most of them do not survive the event so our knowledge about them is limited. The assault is usually carried out Rambo style with an automatic gun in a crowded place, and the assailant usually shoots lots of people and then himself. If he does not kill himself he contrives to have himself shot by the police or army. His final act of destruction and murder is a kind of epitaph, his one big gesture or statement against a society against which he bears a grudge.

In Ireland we have had no real cases of serial killers or mass killers. The cases we have become familiar with usually occurred in the USA, and to a lesser extent in the UK. We have, however, had some offenders who killed two or even three people.

2
RAPISTS

MAN OR MONSTER?

Rape and sexual assault arouse the deepest fears and nightmares of women, who fear that they are becoming not only more numerous but more brutal and heinous. Extensive media coverage of such offences, itself a response to the perceived public appetite for such stories, intensifies the climate of fear. When rape cases come to court, the perpetrator's name is withheld until after conviction. This is to protect his reputation and also the victim's, lest she be recognised through him. In Ireland there is a total ban on reporting the names of offenders in incest cases even after conviction because victims of incest need continuing protection. The public may sometimes feel that the courts go overboard to protect the offender; however, historically, rape has been regarded as a charge easily made and one of the most difficult to defend.

Who are the men (they are almost invariably men) who commit these dreadful crimes? Some people believe they are complete monsters who should be locked up for the rest of their lives, others that they are mad and out of control. The truth is that they are not monsters but ordinary human beings and when one comes in personal contact with them it is not so easy to talk of hanging or castrating them. Neither do they tend to be mentally ill so it is a myth that they are out of control.

Don was in his mid twenties. On this particular night he had been drinking with some friends in a pub in the centre of a large city. They were all quite drunk. During the course of the evening two women, also in their mid twenties, joined the company. Everyone seemed to be having a good time and they drank until closing time. Don and one of the women became friendly during the evening and they went back to her flat for some more drinks. The rest of the group went off in different directions. Don and the woman drank some more and smoked some hash. They started kissing and then things started to go wrong.

Don started to pull at the woman's clothes and wanted her to take them off. She refused and became angry and also afraid. He persisted in trying to remove her blouse and she slapped him and told him he would have to go. Don punched her and continued to remove her clothes by force. The woman was dazed and frightened. She started crying and pleaded with him not to hurt her. Don punched her again and told her to be quiet. Then he raped her. After that he became friendly and insisted that they both have another drink and listen to some more music. They smoked more cigarettes. At that point Don said that they should go to bed and the woman did not object. He was now friendly and reasonable even though he had been out of control and violent a short time before. She was frightened and confused. They went to bed and he wanted to have sex again. She complied because she feared what he might do if she refused or resisted. They were both still drunk but she was sobering up fast. At around four in the morning she slipped out of the bed, got dressed and left. She went to the local police station and reported the rape. The police arrested Don several hours later as he was leaving her flat.

Don pleaded not guilty and maintained that the sex was consensual. He admitted that he and the woman had had sex twice but claimed that she was a willing particip-ant. Both of them had been drunk and he said that his memory of the sex and the later part of the evening was hazy. Her memory was crystal clear. The jury convicted him and he was given a sentence of five years.

This case shows a number of features often found in rape situations. The aggressor was known to the victim, although here the victim got to know the assailant only over the course of the evening. She was not afraid of him during that time and she was happy enough to allow him come back to her flat. He must not have been a 'monster' earlier in the evening and she seems to have quite liked him before the assaults. The victim and the assailant know each other in about 60 per cent of rape offences. Another common feature of rape cases is that the assailant is intoxicated and in 30 per cent of cases the victim is also intoxicated. This does not mean that they were drinking together before the assault although in the above case they clearly were. Another interesting aspect of the above case, and of many cases, is that the aggressor does not under-stand the magnitude of the violence he has perpetrated on the woman. Don felt it was all right for them to go to bed and even have sex again, as if nothing untoward had occurred. The woman cooperated after the first rape because she was terrified that Don would become violent again. She saw what he was capable of and she knew he could seriously injure or even kill her. When Don got up the next day his memory of the events was hazy, a common feature for those with alcohol problems. This further diluted any realisation he might have had of assaulting the woman. Frequently rapists in such situations try to make a date with the woman for the following night!

Rape situations are very varied, as the following examples will show. In the 'van' rape we typically have two young men, often in their early twenties, who have been drinking for several hours. They are usually single but may also be married with children. They decide at some point in the evening that they are going to have some fun and some sex. They cruise around lonely areas such as parks, looking for a young woman. When they spot a suitable target they may drive around to check out a getaway route and to make sure that there is nobody else around. Then they act quickly. The van pulls up beside the unsuspecting victim and she is pulled into the back. The vehicle is then driven away at speed. If the victim struggles at all she is beaten severely by the man who grabbed her and she may even be knocked unconscious.

When the woman comes to, the van is parked in a lonely rural area and she is repeatedly raped by the two drunken men. She may be subjected to all types of indignities such as oral and anal sex as well as beatings.

Nobody will hear her screams and if she does scream the violence in intensified. The men take turns and one may hold the woman down as the other rapes her. If she struggles she may be severely beaten with fists or kicked or head butted. Sometimes men in this situation use objects like metal bars or pieces of wood to beat the victim and may also sexually assault her by inserting such objects, or knives, into her.

Alcohol is a feature here again but it is the adding together of two criminal mentalities that makes a sinister new team. Either man might have been incapable of going so far by himself but each gives the other permission to act out what is in his head and in his fantasy life even though it is one of the ultimate crimes against another human being. They encourage each other, acting as each other's peer support and peer pressure simultaneously. The two together create a monster.

Sometimes this situation progresses to homicide but the more usual conclusion is that the victim is dumped somewhere. She is traumatised, battered and bruised but still alive. If she is not too stunned by the experience she may be able to help the police to find the attackers.

Rapists may be well-off married men or penniless down-and-outs. One of the former type may be the offender in a 'babysit' rape. A teenage girl comes to a couple's house to babysit for the evening. The man may be pleasant and fatherly to her while his wife is around but as soon as she is out of the room he becomes a Romeo. The young woman may be confused by this amorous attention but also a little flattered. She takes no further notice and settles down to watch a video. When the couple returns in the early hours the man insists on leaving her home. Again he is charming and goes out of his way to show concern for her welfare.

On the way home he makes a detour into a secluded park area. The young woman does not know what to do when he starts groping her and trying to kiss her. He may say things like 'I knew you always wanted me' and so on as he overpowers her. She tries to scream but he punches her and orders her to keep quiet. When it is over he returns to being a pleasant fatherly gentleman and they continue on the journey to her home. He treats her almost as if nothing has happened, apart from mentioning their 'little secret'. He even suggests that they do it again some time.

The dreadful dilemma for such a rape victim arises from the fact that her parents and the other couple are friends and have known each other for years. She also has a strange feeling that maybe it was her fault. Has she given him some signal that he misinterpreted? His pleasantness afterwards makes her wonder if she is imagining the horror of what happened. If the young woman can collect herself she will report the attack to her parents and to the police. It she keeps it to herself she or another innocent victim may well be attacked again.

A similar dilemma arises in the case of the young teenager who is raped by a respected person such as a teacher, youth leader or sports coach. Such a person may again know her parents and they in turn may regard highly the commitment and professionalism of the individual involved. The offender may tell the victim that no one will believe her and that it will be her word against his. The impressionable youngster may believe this and be afraid to report the assaults for fear of not being believed or of being blamed for what happened. There may be pressure about such things as the status of the person in the organisation, or anxieties about being selected for the first team. These concerns might well be brushed aside by an adult but they may have great significance for a teenager. Offenders in such privileged positions make full use of their power and control over younger victims. The teenage victim, male or female, may feel powerless. Everyone seems to respect this person and he always seems so nice in other circumstances. This can all be very confusing for the traumatised person. Sometimes it is only year laters that the abused person can summon up courage to make a formal complaint, perhaps as a result of seeing other victims coming forward.

The reaction they get is sometimes less than they expected. If they report to an organisation like a sporting association the association may seem to protect their coach and resist any attempt at an investigation. The injured party may be made to feel like an outlaw and be treated with contempt for daring to sully the name of a respected employee. If their first contact is with the police they usually get a sympathetic ear. However, that may be all they get. If the assaults occurred a number of years before the prosecuting authorities may decide not to prosecute and this leaves the victim in a dreadful position. They are neither vindicated nor is their story aired in court. There is no justice in some of these situations. The victim can be made to feel like a nasty vindictive person who has a grudge against the other person.

Some injured parties decide to take action through the civil courts and sue the offender or the relevant organis- ation. Many of these civil actions are settled out of court so we do not have the same understanding of the success rates for the plaintiffs as we have in the criminal justice system. It is also not clear what makes defendants (the individuals or body against whom the claim is made) and their legal teams fight some cases and settle others before court. For the man in question the biggest issue is usually his reputation but for an organisation it may be money first and reputation or good name second.

The In-Between Offence

Rape has sometimes been called the in-between offence, based on the perception that it lies between homicide and property offences. The commonest types of offences are those against property and the average age of offenders is in the late teens and early twenties. For homicide, the age group is the thirties and forties. The rapist is typically in his mid twenties. Mental illness is very uncommon in property offenders and is present in about 30 per cent of homicide perpetrators. It is uncommon in rapists but more common than in property offenders. The chances of a burglar or shoplifter re-offending is very high whereas the re-offending rate in homicide is extremely low. Rapists are again in between the two with a re-offending rate of about 20 per cent. Offender and victim hardly ever know each other in property offences but almost always do in homicide cases. They know each other in about 30 per cent of rape cases.

Mental illness is uncommon in rapists, occurring in about 5 per cent of cases. The commonest mental illness seen is schizophrenia. The mentally ill man may rape a woman in the context of alcoholic intoxication or, rarely, in the course of another offence such as burglary. One thirty-year-old man with a long history of schizophrenia was living homeless in a city area. He suffered from paranoid delusions and had been admitted to various psychiatric hospitals during the course of the previous year. One evening he broke into an isolated house because he was cold and hungry. He entered the house through a bedroom window and there was an old woman in bed. She screamed and he panicked. He held his hand over her mouth to stop her screaming and then he raped her. He apparently had no intention of committing a sexual offence before he broke into the house. There seems to be a higher incidence of mental illness among men convicted of sexual offences against older women than among rapists in general.

The courts do not have a uniform way of dealing with the mentally ill rapist or sexual offender. Sometimes the view is taken that the man was not fully responsible for his actions so he gets a shorter sentence. This is more likely to occur if it can be shown that the local psychiatric service is willing to admit the person to hospital on a compulsory order for a specified period. These days, fewer and fewer services are willing to do that. The court may also take the view that the rapist who is mentally disturbed and not fully in control of his actions poses a greater threat to the general community. Consequently, judges in such cases impose a very long sentence on the offender. Occasionally the defence of insanity is put forward in rape cases on the basis of the person suffering from a serious mental illness at the time of the incident. This defence is seldom used nowadays because it may mean that the offender will spend an extremely long time in a security hospital.

A manic depressive man may also rape when he is suffering from a pathologically high mood, mania. He is typically full of energy and high spirits. He may be unable to sleep, his thoughts are constantly racing and he must keep chasing around the place. He may become deluded and believe that he is all-powerful and has unlimited resources and money. His libido may be affected so that he has a very much increased sexual appetite. He may also misinterpret social cues and signals and in this context commit a sexual offences such as rape. Courts do not readily accept the explanation that manic people are not in control of themselves so they may receive lengthy sentences. Sexual offences by manic men are rare.

RAPE IN RELATIONSHIPS

Date rape is an issue that worries many women. It usually involves a sexual assault occurring during one of the first few dates with a new partner. The young woman may not know the new boyfriend very well and so she is a little nervous. How much kissing should she allow or how much petting? Both may have had some alcohol and she may feel relaxed because they were having a pleasant time. The young man may have his own views about how far they should go and he may insist on having his way. The young woman is forced to have sex against her will. These situations can develop very quickly and the young woman is left wondering was she to blame for what happened. If the man is confronted or charged with the offence he will claim that it was all consensual and that she knew what she was doing.

Formerly there was a view that a man could not rape his wife because he had sexual rights over her. Now rape within marriage is a criminal offence in most western jurisdictions. A wife has as much right to say 'no' as any other woman. It is no longer acceptable for a drunken husband to return home and force himself on his terrified and disgusted wife. Such women may also be subjected to other forms of physical violence. The police and other caring agencies such as social workers frequently try to protect these victims. They also try to empower them to protect themselves by leaving the man and by making a complaint to the police about the criminal assault. It is very difficult for such a woman to have her husband charged with an offence. She may be afraid of what he might do. She loved the man in the past and may still love him in the present. He is also the father of their children.

We sometimes come across unusual cases where a man rapes and assaults his girlfriend and then her mother. Such an offender may have an abnormal personality or he may be intoxicated by drugs or alcohol at the time of the offence. The assaults may be very violent and fatalities have occurred in such situations. The man often gives a history of sexual fantasies about the mother and his girlfriend but he may also have an angry obsession with the older woman.

THE HOMOSEXUAL RAPIST

Not all rapists are heterosexual men. One young homosexual man in his early twenties had a very bad relationship with his mother. His brothers were married and living away from home and they were both much more successful that he was. He was often unemployed. One afternoon he and his mother argued again. He told her for the first time that he was homosexual and her response was that she wanted him out of the house. He stormed out in fury of resentment and hatred.

He went walking in an area close to where they lived. In waste ground he met a young woman he did not know. Out of the blue he attacked the woman. He started beating and punching her. He sexually assaulted her and when she tried to get away he beat her again. The attack was extremely violent. He raped her and then left her unconscious in the waste ground.

The young man was arrested within hours of the assault and taken into custody. He had no previous history of criminal activity or of violence against anyone. It seems that his longstanding feud with his mother, his anger and his worries about his sexuality all exploded simultaneously on that afternoon and focused on the unknown young woman. He was found guilty of rape and serious assault and given a ten-year sentence.

The more usual homosexual rape situation is where a homosexual man sexually assaults another man and has sex with him against his will. Such rapes are not common occurrences but many may be covered up. It is probably more difficult for a male victim of sexual violence to report the assault than it is for a female victim. The man may fear that he will not be taken seriously by the police. If he is heterosexual he may fear being regarded as a homosexual. If he is homosexual he may fear being stigmatised. It is also very hard for a man to admit that he was unable to protect himself against another man.

Some very savage homosexual rapes are perpetrated against men, and victims of these assaults may take months or years to recover just as in heterosexual rapes. Sometimes the situation is a gang rape where the victim is assaulted and anally or orally penetrated by multiple assailants.

Another setting for homosexual rape is prison, although this seems to be a relatively rare phenomenon in Irish and UK prisons. Some aggressive homosexual men in prisons target and sexually assault younger and weaker young men. In some cases these offenders are heterosexual while outside the prison setting but inside they turn their sexual energies to homosexuality. They are usually aggressive people in all areas of their lives, including their heterosexual relationships.

PROSTITUTES AND OTHER VICTIMS

In recent years we have seen rape trials in which the victim is a prostitute, whereas in the past such actions were seldom seen. One reason was that the woman's previous sexual history would make a successful conviction very unlikely. Another belief was that if a woman is involved in prostitution she is available for sex but at a price. This is a similar to the argument traditionally used in cases of rape within marriage. The man had a right and the woman had no right to say no. It is now recognised that even a prostitute also has a right to say no so if a man forces himself on her he is guilty of rape. Some of the most violent and sadistic rapes and rape-murders are perpetrated on prostitutes. Certain types of men feel that they have a right to treat these women in this way; such men have no respect for women in general and may have a long history of violence against their wives or girlfriends. The prostitute is in an even worse position than the other victims in the perception of the world held by such a man.

A very small number of females are convicted of rape and sexual assaults against other women. Such assaults may involve the woman assisting a male offender in committing a sexual act. She would then normally be found guilty of aiding and abetting the male, who is usually the principal offender. The court is entitled to impose the full sentence on the woman as if she were guilty of the main offence. Sometimes we see cases where one woman or more decides to sexually assault another woman because of some argument or feud. Such a woman or women may arrange to have a male friend commit the sexual acts and she may take part in the assault by helping the man. These assailants are often aggressive and disturbed women with a criminal lifestyle.

Some male sexual offenders have individual way of operating and carrying out their crimes. They may target particular types of women and follow them, always waiting for an opportunity to strike. An offender may call at the door of the designated victim and try to gain access by pretending to be a gas man or some other official. Such a perpetrator may present himself very well and the woman may be completely fooled. Once inside the offender is free to carry out his crimes undisturbed.

Most victims of rape are women in their teens and twenties but rapists may also target elderly women, sometimes using burglary as the the pretext for entering the house of the victim he has already identified. Rape is extremely traumatic for any victim but it is a particularly horrendous ordeal for the elderly, some of whom never get over the assault.

The commonest ways for men accused of rape to defend themselves in court is to claim that the assault did not occur at all or to say that they had sex but it was with the woman's consent. The issue then becomes one person's word against that of another. If there is conclusive forensic evidence such as semen establishing that in fact sex took place and medical evidence that force was used, the jury may well convict. However, if there is no evidence of bruising or other injuries the jury has a more difficult job. If a woman is terrified during an attack she may be wise to comply with the attacker's wishes in order to avoid serious violence. This is still a rape but there would be no medical evidence of a struggle. If the attacker is a stranger to her it is likely that the jury will accept her story but if he is a friend they may be more dubious.

Sometimes – but rarely – women make false allegations of rape and sexual assault. Such allegations may be made by a mentally ill woman who has delusions about being raped but this is very rare indeed.

Can Anything be Done for the Offenders?
This is a question that is often asked and many groups demand that rapists have therapy in prisons. It is known

that about 20 per cent of rapists re-offend so anything that would help them and reduce re-offending rates would be good for all society. Unfortunately, only a minority feel that they have a problem or are in need of any help. One of the major disorders seen in those convicted of rape is alcoholism. In about 60 per cent of rapes the assailant is intoxicated at the time of the offence and most of these offenders have alcohol problems. I often ask the person charged with a sexual offence: 'If you had not been drinking that night, would we be talking to each other now?' The answer is almost invariably 'No'.

A very small proportion of those convicted of sexual offences have a mental illness such a schizophrenia and need ongoing treatment for their illness in prison or in a psychiatric hospital. It is vital for these individuals that the treatment be continued even after they leave the prison system. Sadly, they may be lost to all caring agencies at this point.

Sexual suppressant medication may be helpful in a proportion of rapists but is not widely used. Public opinion became very concerned about the civil liberty issue involved with interfering with a person's sexual drive and his consent to such treatment. A small number of offenders have a serious problem controlling their sexuality and such medication can help cut down the sexual drive for a period or in the long term. This form of medication may be more commonly used in the management of sexual offenders in the future.

Many rapists have problems around anger and violence. Some of them have serious problems in their attitudes to women and a history of violence in their relationships and sexual activity which made the lives of their spouses or partners a misery.

Psychotherapy in prison or in the community can be helpful for a proportion of sexual offenders, especially if they seek help before any serious offence takes place. It is more normal, however, for them to be chosen for such therapy after they are charged with an offence and for them to avail of therapy before, during or after prison. Such psychotherapy may involve individual work with a therapist but it is usually more productive in a group setting with other offenders. This work helps the offender to look at his own sexuality and the offending behaviour. He is also helped to examine his violent tendencies in general and his attitude to women in particular. The success rate depends on the offender's willingness and ability to cooperate. It is unfortunate that only about 20 per cent of rapists are interested in availing of such services.

EXHIBITIONISTS

The offence of indecent exposure occurs when a man exposes his genitals to a female in a public place. There is no corresponding offence for women. If such a man seeks psychiatric help for a repeated urge to expose himself his condition is called exhibitionism. It is the commonest of all sex offences and most females report that they have been exposed to it at some point during their lives.

Indecent exposure is often regarded as an offence of no great consequence. In recent years professionals involved in crime, sexual crime in particular, have seriously questioned this complacent view, for two reasons. The first is that many women or girls who are victimised by a flasher are traumatised by the experience, a trauma similar to that suffered by the rape victim. The second concerns the risk of the exhibitionist committing a more serious sexual assault such as rape. It is known that about 5 per cent of indecent exposers go on to commit rape and a proportion of these rapes take place during an episode of indecent exposure. About 20 per cent of rapists have a history of exposing themselves to women prior to committing rape. The indecent exposers who seem to be most likely to commit a more serious sexual assault are those who try to make verbal or physical contact with the victim or victims. Those who have an erect penis or who actively masturbate during an incident are also more likely to commit a more serious assault. There is, therefore, ample evidence that we should take indecent exposure seriously.

Exhibitionists expose themselves because they have an urge to commit the act which they find more and more difficult to control. Many offenders say that their problem started in their late teens and occurred at different times during their lives. Frequently exhibitionists say that the urge is more frequent when they are going through periods of stress in their lives, involving for instance marital difficulties or problems at work. There is usually a lead-up period of a few days where the man feels the mounting tension and urge and then the release of the tension by the act itself. Some report feeling exhilarated during the act but then feeling deflated or a little depressed or guilty afterwards. At a later point, perhaps days or weeks later, the process starts again.

This whole process is similar to the impulse of the compulsive female shoplifter and some experts have suggested that these are expressions of the same tendency in the two sexes. They both report a cycle of mounting tension and an urge to act, which is more frequent and intense during periods of stress. The tension reaches a climax in the act itself; thereafter the individual feels an anticlimax of low mood and even guilt. In both situtations the offenders seem to commit the offence until they are caught. They experience some pleasure in being apprehended which is hard to understand.

The pattern of exposing is often very specific to the individual. Some men expose themselves only in particular parks or from their cars. Others prefer built-up areas. For some, the time of the day – late at night or very early in the morning – is important. Some like to expose themselves from their own front window, a feature that will make detection very likely. Amazingly, people who know such an offender may tolerate his behaviour for decades and not make a complaint to the police.

For most exhibitionists the type of victim is important. Some expose only to schoolgirls in a group while others perform only in front of lone young females. A small number of offenders expose themselves to women who know them and others confine their activities to elderly women.

A small proportion of exhibitionists are mentally ill and suffer from schizophrenia or a depressive illness at the time of the incident. Yet again, as with other sexual offenders, the commonest associated problem observed in these people is alcoholism. A proportion of offences occur during alcoholic intoxication. Some alcoholic exhibitionists expose themselves during periods of drinking as well as periods of sobriety.

Can anything be done to help these men and prevent re-offending? As ever, this depends on the individual accepting that there is a problem and being willing to do something about it. If he has alcohol problems they need to be addressed, as they may be the main contributing factor. If there are marital problems a professional agency may help the couple to deal more effectively with them. The rare case of real mental illness will require an offender to seek help from his local psychiatric services. If the man has sexual problems, such as feelings of inadequacy, some psychotherapy may be of benefit. It has often been suggested that exhibitionists have a subconscious urge to frighten the female victim with their penis in order to prove to themselves that they are real men. The urges of some offenders may be so strong that they need the help of sexual suppressant medication for a period.

In some cases of indecent exposure, where the offenders do not have a long history of offending, being charged and appearing in court can be so traumatic and frightening that they never repeat the offence.

3
CHILD SEXUAL ABUSERS

THE PAEDOPHILE

The paedophile is nearly always a male whose main sexual orientation is towards children. He would recognise his attraction to children from his teens when his sexuality is maturing. Paedophilia is a sexual orientation just like heterosexuality or homosexuality. It is not a disease or a mental illness. Paedophilia is not a danger to children in itself, it is only a problem when the man decides to act on his sexual desires and abuse children. The case histories of these men have many similarities.

Gerard was in his early thirties, single and living alone. His mother had died when he was in his early twenties and he still missed her. There was never a close relationship between him and his father, who had died several years earlier. During the day Gerard worked in his own small grocery shop. He had had a small number of girlfriends over the years but he had no sexual interest in women although he enjoyed female company. In his early twenties he had tried sex with prostitutes and with some girlfriends but he felt little sexual arousal or interest. He had a number of male friends and had had brief homosexual relationships with some of these during his twenties. These encounters made him realise that he was not completely homosexual in sexual orientation or at least not primarily interested in adult men.

From his late teens Gerard realised that his main sexual orientation was towards male children. There was a number of episodes in his mid-teens where Gerard and other boys mutually masturbated. He knew that this type of activity interested him more with younger boys than with the older ones. His fantasy life, during masturbation or even during normal activity, almost exclusively focused on young boys around the ages of nine to eleven.

As he grew into adulthood this sexual interest in boys strengthened and he knew that he had no real sexual interest in adult men or women. Neither had he any interest in female children. When he walked down the street he would look at young boys and fantasise about what it would be like to touch them, kiss them and have sex with them. Gerard knew that having sex with a young boy was legally wrong so he refrained from acting on his sexual desires and drives. But when he reached his early thirties he decided to see how far he could go and get away with it.

There was a boy of ten who often came into his shop with whom Gerard got on well. Gerard found him very attractive because of his dark colouring and strong build. He felt that the boy was not well cared for at home so he decided to start giving him attention. The first approach was to ask him to come around after school to help out in the shop. The boy was delighted with this and soon he was in the shop every afternoon. Gerard always rewarded the boy generously with money and sweets and the child enjoyed the attention and became dependent on it.

Gerard knew the boy's parents and they were happy with the arrangement. The father had a drink problem and was seldom at home. The boy's mother was under a lot of pressure because she had six other children in the family and there were marital difficulties related to her husband's alcoholism. The afternoon job for the boy seemed like a fine idea to the parents whenever they thought about it. It also meant a little more money. They never suspected anything about Gerard's interest in their son.

He decided to get closer to the boy so he invited him into his living room one evening after closing the shop. His first plan was for them to watch a video. The boy was happy to comply and they both started to watch the video, which had some sexual scenes in it. Gerard encouraged the boy to talk about sex and then suggested that they learn more about the topic by examining each other's genitals. This progressed to fondling and mutual mastur- bation. The boy did not seem too put out by this and was very happy when he was given extra money. Gerard warned him that he must not tell anyone about their little secret and he even made him swear an oath. The boy was a little confused but he also felt happy and special.

These sessions went on several times per week over a number of years. Sometimes they involved oral sex and on a few occasions Gerard attempted to have anal inter- course with the boy. He always gave him money and also made sure to renew their vow of secrecy. When the boy was about sixteen he decided to stop going to the shop because he did not want to continue with the sexual activity. He kept his silence about the abuse.

Gerard persuaded the child to allow him to videotape their sessions on several occasions and he used these videos to stimulate himself when alone. One of his male friends was also a paedophile and he became very excited about the video when Gerard showed it to him. He invited Gerard to a session with him and another boy and they both abused the boy while having the scene recorded on videotape.

When his first boy left, Gerard decided to befriend another young boy who often came in to the shop after school. The process started over again. He persuaded this boy to bring a friend and he found that he was able to increase the number of victims while carefully making sure that they would keep their silence like the first boy. He achieved this by a combination of sweets, money, threats and making the boy swear oaths.

The sexual offences of the paedophile may start in the late teens and continue throughout his life. Approximately 40 per cent of these men are heterosexual paedophiles, 40 per cent are homosexual paedophiles and 20 per cent are bisexual paedophiles. A small percentage get married and have children of their own. Some of this relatively rare group may abuse their own children; others do not. In general they remain single as they have no sexual interest in adult women.

Apart from paedophile offences such men tend not to have a criminal history. This is in contrast to the rapist, who may have a criminal background and also a history of convictions for violence. Relatively few paedophiles have a serious alcohol problem, whereas approximately 60 per cent of rapists have. Mental illness, such as schizophrenia or serious depression, is no more common in paedophiles than in the general population, whereas it is slightly more common in rapists.

The cycle of abuse is often repeated over and over again in the same format by the offender. He may engage the child in games, educational projects, trips to the cinema or elsewhere. There follow gentle attempts to encourage the child to get closer to him both emotionally and physically. Frequently the adult will give the child enticements such as sweets, money and presents. This process can take days or weeks to complete. The child feels important and usually enjoys the attention. Abusers frequently target children who do not seem to be getting much attention from other, more appropriate sources. The offender may simultaneously gain the trust and confidence of the parents or others, such as people in charge of a school or youth club, depending on the particular situation. He may be seen as a caring and considerate individual who is very good with children.

The abuse itself usually starts by touching and fondling. The child may be encouraged to touch the man sexually. Pornographic books or films may be used to encourage this process. Occasionally, abusers use alcohol or sedative medication to intoxicate the child to aid the assaults. As time goes on the abuse becomes more intense with mutual masturbation, digital penetration and later oral, vaginal or anal intercourse. The frequency of the activity varies, some victims being abused on a daily basis, others monthly or even less often.

The frequency of the abuse is important in terms of the effects it will have on the victim. The once-off episode of abuse tends normally to be less traumatic, and the greater the number of episodes the greater the trauma. The child may not know the abuser and the once-off episode may be short-lived. The abuse that more commonly comes to the attention of the authorities is the longer-term abuse where the man and the child know each other well and the abuse is systematic. This is the form of sexual abuse that normally causes more serious emotional damage. However, from time to time, the once-off type of abuse can be horrific, with full penetrative abuse and even murder.

Most paedophiles focus on particular age groups because of their sexual preference. The commonest age group to be abused is between nine and eleven for boy and girls. Some offenders target only particular types of children such as blonde or dark, or they may focus on the unhappy and apparently lonely child. A small number of offenders seem to assault only very young children such as in the range between two and four. Some abuse even younger children.

The control of the child is something at which most paedophiles are very adept from the beginning of their careers. An interesting and subtle method is for the abuser to make the child think that their special secret is so important that they need to take a solemn vow of silence about it all. If the child were to break this solemn vow he would be committing a sin or similar serious transgression. The most important weapon used by the abuser is fear. He tells the child that if he or she tells anyone about what went on the authorities will send him, the abuser, to prison but they will also send the child away to a home. This idea can frighten a child into remaining silent for a very long time. The man may also threaten to kill the child or his or her family. Very few children can withstand that kind of pressure.

How do abusers justify their actions to themselves and to others when they are caught? The excuses that are used by people who sexually interfere with children are similar the world over. Some offenders say that their only fault is that they love children too much. Others say that they were educating the child about sexuality and about growing up. Some offenders say that their reason for abusing a child was to warn him about sexual abuse and child abusers!

An interesting quasi-legal argument that is sometimes put forward by child abusers is firstly that they, as paedophiles, are morally entitled to express their sexuality. They also deny that sexual abuse is damaging to anyone. The second limb of that argument is that a child is entitled to the love, including the sexual love, of a caring adult. Some abusers try to strengthen their argument by pointing out the fact that paedophile activity was acceptable to some extent in Greek and Roman times. Few adults would describe sexual abuse of children as something useful. It is hard to imagine that any parent would see the abuse of their child by a paedophile as a relationship which is loving or caring. Adult survivors of child sexual abuse usually describe how damaging the attentions of the abuser were and how difficult it is to recover from that damage.

CHILD PORNOGRAPHY AND PROSTITUTION

Child pornography is a topic that is often in the news and rightly causes concern. There were concerns in recent years that during 'snuff' movies some children were murdered just for entertainment. The corrupting influence of the pornography itself is important, whether it is magazines or videos, but the children in the pictures are being abused in the production of these products. This makes child pornography quite different from the adult variety. When adult models or actors decide to involve themselves in pornographic productions they are usually over the age of consent and are capable of deciding what they want to do. Children are not legally capable of this rational decision making because they are too young. There appears to be a growing market for child pornography on the the World Wide Web on the Internet.

Child prostitution is a topic that causes revulsion in most people. How could a person allow a child to be abused in order to make money? It seems that some people in countries such as Thailand and the Philippines are prepared to allow this to happen. In some areas this has become a highly organised form of tourism and local economies are often dependent on this trade. Many countries are introducing laws to enable police forces in the home countries to charge people who are involved in child sexual abuse in other jurisdictions. In some areas it is reported that it is possible to buy a child. This is an incomprehensible idea to most normal people. It is feared that some of these bought children may end up being murdered for sexual pleasure.

Child prostitutes in any area of the world face the same problems as adult prostitutes, as indeed do all those people who are sexually abused. These include unwanted pregnancies and disease. Pregnancy in the child may end the child's life, as may a cheap and incompetent abortion. The diseases that these children run the risk of contracting are HIV/AIDS, Hepatitis B or C, and other diseases that can be transmitted sexually such as gonorrhoea and syphilis. Many incur physical injuries because of sexual abuse by adults and they may also be injured by gratuitous violence from offender holidaymakers or the pimps who control the business.

Special Categories of Abusers

The profession which has come in for most criticism in this area in recent years are Catholic priests and religious. The church itself has been criticised for what was seen by many as an inadequate and tardy response. Priests have traditionally been in a very special, privileged and powerful position in most countries worldwide. They have been seen as men of God who are usually good people in themselves. They say masses, baptise children and forgive sin. They were almost the only group who had unquestioned access to children in the church, in the community and in people's homes. Nobody was suspicious of their contact with children in schools and institutions of all kinds, including hospitals. How could such men abuse children?

When children reported that a priest abused them there was disbelief in every quarter. Teachers, parents and the church refused to take these complaints seriously. Priests just did not do such things. It has only relatively lately been realised that no group is incapable of abusing children. There were reports of abuse by clerics in schools, in the community and in all areas that priests and religious have contact with children. It cannot be emphasised enough that these abusers represent only a very small percentage of the clergy in general.

The church's response was always perceived as covering up the problem. The offending cleric would be moved to another area in the hope that the problem would not recur. He would go to confession, confess his sins and be forgiven. His colleagues prayed that he would change his ways. Sadly, this simplistic view of paedophilia played right into the hands of the offender, who was set free to start all over again in a new area. The church authorities did not seem to think of the child safety implications for the new area or position.

The church tried to deal with the problem internally. Traditionally such a massive organisation with almost unlimited resources was able to deal with any problem which came its way. It could deal with hunger and education in third world countries and even arrange for medical care for large communities. Paedophilia was a problem that the church did not understand; nor did it fully comprehend the strength of the public response to child abuse as an issue. Senior church people found it very hard to accept that there was some problem which was bigger than the organisation and capable of damaging it severely. The church was traditionally concerned about priests having relationships with women and perhaps thought of homosexuality and child abuse as minor aberrations. It is only in relatively recent times that senior church people have been able to focus fully on the victim's experience in the whole debate about child sexual abuse. Compensation and money have also come into the picture internationally and sometimes people felt that the church was interested in that aspect to the exclusion of other issues. Victims are now saying that they want to be acknowledged as victims and many also feel that they are entitled to compensation for having been wronged and traumatised.

In February 1996, the Irish Catholic bishops produced a document which gives guidelines for the action that should be taken by the church when allegations are made against priests and religious. It was generally welcomed by all the agencies because the bishops firmly tried to put children and victims at the top of the priority list. The general principle is also accepted that all cases of allegations of sexual abuse should be reported to the garda and civil authorities for investigation.

Other professional groups have come under scrutiny and pressure in the child sexual abuse area. Some teachers, sports coaches, doctors and others have been investigated. People who look after children in homes or institutions and in social organisations are all in sensitive positions now. This means that they have to carefully examine how they operate professionally because they are under scrutiny as people who have a privileged and powerful position with children and who work in very close contact with them. The vast majority of these people are trying to do their best to help children in the educational, sport and leisure areas. There is a new climate of fear which has been caused, as in the church, by a very small group of wrongdoers.

Young sexual offenders are a group that cause many headaches for the child protection agencies and the professionals who deal with abusers. These are typically sixteen-year-old boys who sexually abuse a neighbour's five- or six-year-old child. Often this type of offending occurs during babysitting but it can occur in any context. The parents of the victim may try to ignore what the child is telling them as they are unable to accept that their child was abused by the nice teenager they have been using for babysitting. The child may mention something about the funny games that the older boy played or mention something about holding the teenager's 'willie'. These situations cause enormous problems between neighbours, with both families immediately on a war footing. The correct action for the parents of the child is to report their concerns to the community care authorities in the area or the police. If the child has been abused he or she needs counselling and help with recovery. The family also needs support.

The difficulties that this offender poses for the author-ities are considerable. Should he be allowed to remain in his own home where the victim and the victim's family will see him every day? If there are other young children around what should be done to protect them? Is he a danger to younger brothers and sisters in his own house? The longer-term headache is the issue of whether the sixteen-year-old offender is a teenager exploring and experimenting with sex or a young paedophile? Only time will answer that question. If the authorities arrange to have him moved to a hostel for a period, which hostel will take a young sexual offender?

In the past the first reaction to the young sexual offender tended to be that he must be a victim himself and that he needed help with that area of his life. Interestingly enough, he is only a little more likely to have been abused than the ordinary teenager. The majority of these offenders were never abused. It is now accepted by professionals that he must firstly be regarded as an abuser in order that the protection of other children is put top of the agenda. *His* needs as a possible victim and as an abuser come second.

Not all child abusers are male. Female paedophiles are rare but they do exist. These are often disturbed women who are angry at children or men for some reason. Occasionally, one sees such women getting sexual pleasure from sexually interfering with children but their motivation is more likely to be related to causing pain. Some women are convicted of paedophile offences because they have aided and abetted males who committed offences against children. A rare situation is where a mother allows her daughter to be abused for money. Such women may be abused and dominated themselves, sometimes by a pimp. One woman said that she allowed her daughter to be raped by the child's stepfather as a punishment because she was a naughty girl.

Can paedophiles be helped in any way or is it all hopeless? Their sexuality is fixed, so efforts at changing this aspect of their make-up is of no value. About 20 per cent of paedophiles recognise that it is unacceptable to abuse children sexually because it damages them physically and emotionally. These individual are amenable to individual or group therapy which helps them to examine their own sexuality and the offending itself. They often go through a 'cycle' or pattern in their offending and they are helped to look at that. This may help them to recognise this pattern and avoid the behaviour in the future. It is also vital to help them to understand the victim's experience and the damage that sexual abuse can do to children and adults. A proportion of paedophiles benefit from sexual suppressant medication to cut down their sexual drive either in the short or long term. This can now be offered in oral or injectable forms. The main difficulty with medication is that very few paedophiles want their sexual drive to be interfered with.

INCEST OFFENDERS

Incest means unlawful sexual relationships within families. The commonest form that is reported to the authorities is father-daughter incest abuse. This is usually the most damaging type of sexual abuse for victims, for two reasons. The first is that the abuser is the child's father who is normally expected by children to be a protector and a person who loves them. The second reason is that the child is a captive victim with no hope of escape. Consequently the abuse may go on over a very long time. Most children know that they can rely on their parents if there is a problem but who do you go to if the assailant is your father? The mother in these situations may be a victim in other ways and even if the child tells her, she may be afraid to act. Such a woman may be terrified of the husband's violence. She may fear losing the husband for emotional or financial reasons. Many of these families have very low incomes and if the man were to leave, their financial situation would be even worse.

In about 50 per cent of cases the abusing father has a serious alcohol problem. The abuse may start in the setting of intoxication but usually continues afterwards even when he is sober. Children may remember the smell of the drunken father as he gets into bed beside them after coming home from the pub. A child may be afraid to wake anyone else because the father has threatened her and warned her to stay quiet. Some alcoholic fathers say that they cannot remember abusing their children because of alcoholic memory blackouts. If this is the case it is difficult to do any useful therapeutic work with them. Many men who claim they cannot remember the abuse are fooling themselves or trying to fool the interviewer.

Like the paedophile, the abusing father plans carefully how to keep the child from telling anyone. A common way is to threaten to hit or even kill the child. Other fathers use sweets, money or other bribes. Some fathers tell the child that if they tell anyone about the abuse, daddy will be taken to prison and the child will be put into an orphanage. The child is frequently made to feel guilty and responsible for what is going on. Many victims carry this guilt throughout their lives.

Fathers and stepfathers use various excuses and justifications as to why they abused their children. A common explanation is, 'My main problem, doctor, is that I loved my children too much.' Others say they were educating the child or preparing them for adult sex and marriage. Some even say they were showing them what sexual abuse was like so they would recognise it if it occurred! A number of these men say that the child was responsible. They claim that she knew what she was doing and that she must have been having sex with other men before she seduced the father. A small number of men say that their wives would not have sex with them so they had no option but have sex with their children. An interesting variation is: 'I only abused my own children, I would never interfere with anyone else's.'

Many incestuous fathers are inept men with poor social skills who come across as passive and diffident. A smaller number are aggressive and domineering. This latter group are more likely to have treated their wives badly as well. The whole household may be afraid of such a man. However, very few incest offenders have a past criminal history of any kind. A sad thing about these situations is that in some cases the abusing father may be good to his children in other areas of their relationship. The children may love their father for most of the time but hate the abusing aspect of his activities. This causes difficulties for the victim when he or she has to think about reporting the case and later giving evidence in court. They may feel that they are responsible for sending their daddy to prison and splitting up the family. Of course it is the perpetrator himself who is responsible for this. Such children may hate and love the father at the same time.

People outside the family, and even professionals, can sometimes find it difficult to understand this dilemma for the victim. But the assailant in these cases is the child's father, the only father the child will ever have. The sad victim probably has conflicting feelings about the offender and may be emotionally pulled in different directions. There is a similar dilemma for the mother.

A mother is sometimes blamed for not taking action when she knew what was going on. This is usually a very unfair judgement because we never fully know what pressures she is under in particular situations. A vital part of the process of investigation, child protection and therapy in these cases is the counselling and support of the mother. In approximately 50 per cent of incest cases the mother totally rejects the husband and sides with the child. The marriage usually ends at that point. The other 50 per cent of mothers take a less decisive course and try to support the husband and the child. Occasionally it is the child who is rejected and not believed. This is a dreadful position for the child victim.

False accusations of incest offending do occur but they are rare. One area where false accusations of abuse are made is where there are judicial separation proceedings and there is a lot of acrimony between the husband and wife. This is rare but recognised internationally as a modern day reality. The false accusation of sexual abuse is used against the father to prevent him having access to the children. In such situations the children are being used as pawns in the parents' dispute. The man's reputation is also being destroyed maliciously.

In many respects the pattern of incest offending by fathers tends to be very stereotyped. In sexual offender clinics one hears the same story over and over again from different men. The commonest age of the victim is between nine and eleven. Rare cases are seen where a child as young as a few months old is abused. The abuse usually starts with touching or inappropriate kissing. Some offenders encourage the child to look at pornographic material, whether in magazines or videos, and to talk about sexual matters. The abuse progresses to overt sexual fondling which may include penetration by fingers. This is often followed by sexual intercourse. Frequently the abuser makes the child masturbate him. Oral sex is a common part of incest abuse and many children find this the most traumatic. Anal penetration is less common but it does occur.

The pattern is similar to the paedophile's cycle of offending in many respects. However, fathers seem in general only to abuse within their own families, although there are exceptions to this. These men have usually had a reasonable heterosexual relationship and marriage and the offending starts when the child or children are approaching puberty. It is as if they are mostly heterosexual but the paedophile part of their personalities emerges at this later point in their own families. Alcohol problems are also much more common in the incestuous father than in the paedophile.

Daughters are more commonly abused by their fathers but the homosexual abuse of boys by their fathers also occurs. International figures suggest that 60 per cent of the victims of father incest abuse are girls and 40 per cent boys. Our experience at the Central Mental Hospital, where we have run a sexual offender clinic since April 1989, is that the abuse of sons is much less common, but we feel that there may be a real problem with under-reporting. The abuse of boys follows the same pattern as the girls with kissing and fondling progressing to more serious abuse. The traumatic effects, both short-term and long-term, are the same for boys and girls. With boys there may be the added issue of the child's maturing sexuality and sexual orientation. Many boys who are abused wonder for years if they are homosexual or not. They may have serious problems in heterosexual relationships for a very long time because of this doubt.

In general these offences are committed by men but in a tiny minority of cases, around one per cent, there is involvement of the mother. Nearly all of the cases I have come across involved the mother aiding and abetting the father or stepfather to abuse her child or children. Internationally there seems to be little information about this area of offending.

The frequency of offending by fathers can be anything from daily to monthly. Some children have to endure penetrative and nasty abuse on a daily basis for years. In a small number of cases the abuse continues from childhood, say from eight years of age, into the twenties. The location may remain the same, for instance the child's bedroom or the parents' bedroom when the mother is out of the house. A common time for abuse is late at night when everyone else is asleep. Incest abuse can take place anywhere, including outdoors or in garden sheds.

The usual situation is that the eldest girl is abused first from around the age of nine until she is about fourteen. Stepchildren are more at risk of abuse. The man abuses the first child until the next girl is around the age of eight or nine and he may then switch to the younger child. This process can progress through the family. Less often one comes across cases where the abuser offends against several children in the family over the same period of time. This can mean different children on different days or even several children at the same time. In a small number of cases children may be abused by their father and also by their grandfather.

SIBLING INCEST OFFENDERS

The next commonest group of incest offenders is brothers who abuse their sisters. The usual situation is that at fifteen or sixteen a brother sexually abuses a younger sister. The victim in these cases is normally a girl from about eight up to fourteen. The abuse often starts out with a certain amount of play and even apparent consent by the girl but frequently the sexual activity is forced on her. She wants to stop but the older and stronger brother insists. Such abuse may occur on a few occasions only but in some cases it can go on for years. Being abused by one's father is usually the most traumatic type of incest abuse but some women's lives have been totally ruined by repeated sexual abuse by a brother.

A rare situation is where a brother and sister choose to continue an incestuous relationship into adulthood. Such people may have been abused as children but not necessarily so. They may both be immature individuals who have difficulty relating to other people. Such a couple may depend enormously on each other for emotional support and care, and they may see nothing wrong with what they are doing. Incest of this kind is illegal in our society but not, interestingly, in all societies. It is difficult to persuade such people to change their lifestyle.

The homosexual abuse of one brother by another is a lot less frequent than brother and sister abuse. This homosexual abuse can also be very traumatic for the victim, who may carry the emotional scars for life. As in other forms of male homosexual abuse the victim may have problems concerning his sexual orientation throughout his life. A rare form of sibling incest abuse is where the teenage abuser abuses multiple siblings, boys and girls, in his own family. Such offenders tend to have very disturbed personalities and sometimes exhibit early signs of mental illness.

What part does abuse in the offender's own childhood play in the development of sexual offending? In the younger offender, such as the sibling offender, it seems to be more important than in the case of the father incest offender. Most paedophiles and adult incest offenders are no more likely to have been sexually abused in childhood than the general population. The national average figures for childhood sexual abuse lies somewhere between 5 per cent and 15 per cent, depending on what source you use. Adult child sexual abusers have a history of being abused themselves in the same proportion. Some mentally handicapped individuals who were abused as children go on to abuse in the same way that they were abused, as if they had learned an abusing cycle, but this is very rare.

It seems most likely that the paedophile and the adult incest offender are constitutionally paedophile in their sexually orientation but to different degrees. The incest offender has mixed heterosexual and paedophile orientations. The sibling offender may also be more likely to have been abused himself but only in a proportion of cases.

Cases of sibling offending are not commonly seen in the courts. One of the reasons for this is that perpetrators are often seen as victims themselves. This may or may not be true, depending on the circumstance. Some are young paedophiles. Another group are aggressive young men victimising their younger siblings. Some are immature boys who are experimenting sexually. In any case, they should probably be seen as abusers first and the issue of the protection of the victim and other vulnerable children should be put first on the agenda. This may mean putting the offender out of the house or even into the care of the local authority. The problem of their own victimisation, if it is relevant, and counselling for this, should come second.

Child Protection and Therapy for Offenders

The first principle in child physical abuse and child sexual abuse is the protection of the child. This obviously includes protection of all other children in a family setting and in the extended family. Professionals may have to think of a wider net of protection that could include neighbours' children or children in a nearby playschool or similar context. The community care team in a local area is usually central to this process. Social workers and other professionals investigate complaints and make decisions about risks to children and about how to deal with the problem.

One of the first issues is to separate the child from the offender. If the offender is the father, the first approach is to ask him to leave the house. The mother may need encouragement to support this request. If he refuses, the authorities may be forced to consider arranging to have the children taken into care to a safe place. Such an action is never lightly undertaken and usually requires a court order.

The next step is normally to inform the police in order that the criminal justice aspects of the case can be investigated and acted upon. The prosecuting authorities in the jurisdiction then decide whether to prosecute or not. This decision may take weeks or months to make. Some of the issues that are taken into account are the age of the child and his or her reliability as witness, the presence of medical or forensic evidence and how long ago the abuse is alleged to have taken place. If the accused person makes a statement, this is also taken into account.

When all the investigations have been completed, therapy for the child is arranged. This may be with a local child guidance clinic or with a specialised child sexual abuse centre. The mother is usually offered support but there are very few organised programmes for mothers in this type of situation. There is a growing need for such services to counsel and support such forgotten victims. They need to be empowered to decide about such issues as protecting their children, the future of the marriage and their own future. Individual cases are usually handled by social workers or other professionals but support groups and counselling services tend to be *ad hoc* rather than planned and integrated.

The next issue is therapy for the abusers. Only 50 per cent of fathers accused of incest admit they have a problem and accept counselling. As with any sexual offender, if they do not admit guilt one can do very little for them. Central to any therapeutic work that is done with these father incest offenders is the attempt to help them look at the bizarre ways of perceiving their abuse of their own children. The therapeutic process aims at helping the abusers to change their ways of looking at the abusive situation. They also need to look at their own sexuality and the paedophile component of it that they may have denied all their lives. The most important function of the therapeutic process is that they start to appreciate the victim's experience and his or her trauma.

Therapeutic work with sexual offenders is usually best done in a group setting, incestuous fathers with similar offenders, offending brothers with other young sexual offenders. Other members of such a group might be of the 'babysitter' type. In a group setting, offenders are encouraged to challenge each other and to point out how they may be deceiving people around them, and deceiving themselves, about their offending. The therapist encourages this process and keeps the discussions focused on the relevant topics and case histories. Useful work can also be done with offenders on a one to one basis but these people are often so manipulative that the group therapy model is usually preferred. Therapy may go on over eighteen months or two years.

Mental illness is very rare among abusing fathers and sons but it does occur. The man may be suffering from depression or a schizophrenic episode at the time of the offence. Such individuals are usually regarded as mentally ill rather than incest offenders and they are treated as patients by the psychiatric services in the normal way. Alcohol problems are quite common among abusing fathers and about 50 per cent of them are alcoholic. This problem needs to be brought under control before any useful work can be done with the abuse problem. Some offenders are dry alcoholics who have spent years in Alcoholics Anonymous. These can be very good at group therapy work because of the AA experience.

Sexual suppressant medication may be helpful to many sexual offenders, including incest offenders. Such medication can be given in tablet form and more recently in a long-acting injectable form. This gets over the problem of non-compliance with medication which is common among sexual offenders.

It is generally thought that sexual offender programmes in prisons and in the community can help to reduce re-offending among known offenders but it is difficult to get hard figures about this. The issue of how to measure re-offending is debatable in its own right. Re-conviction rates are important put probably represent only the tip of the iceberg. Most sexual abuse of all kinds goes unreported and it is thought that only about five per cent of complaints of child sexual abuse result in conviction. There is a shortage of information at this point about the long-term impact of offender programmes but practitioners are hopeful that it is possible to help the motivated offender to change.

A useful new approach to the problem of child abuse, including child sexual abuse, is to increase awareness through classroom teaching. A 'Stay Safe Programme' has been operating in most Irish primary schools for a number of years. The central message for the child is that they are entitled not to be abused and if they are abused or afraid they should say 'No', try to get away, and tell a parent or teacher.

4

ARSONISTS

'C'mon, baby, light my fire' (1967)
Jim Morrison 1943-71

Arson is an ancient and frightening crime. It usually involves damage to property by fire but may also result in violence to animals or humans. Fire-setting is a term that is sometimes used, as is pyromania. The fire can be as trivial as one in a small wastepaper basket which is easily brought under control or as catastrophic as a blaze that destroys a block of flats, killing many people or destroys a factory or warehouse causing millions of pounds worth of damage. All fires can be caused by a single match and can be started by a child or a hardened vicious criminal. The arsonist is often the most feared of offenders because he can commit his crime so easily and with so little preparation. The fire he sets may literally envelop a family while they sleep. Even though people are usually killed by fumes rather than flames, the fear of being burned alive runs deep in most people's subconscious.

Ken never really fitted in. He was the younger of two boys. His parents split up when he was six and the rest of his childhood was unhappy. His brother seemed to fare better as he was brighter and more sociable. Ken tended to be a loner and to live in his own fantasy world. He was not successful academically and remembers being bullied and laughed at by more able classmates. He just retreated more into himself, angry and lonely.

When he was fourteen he went out one night with some petrol in a can. The can was kept in the shed at home for the lawnmower. He hated the school, the teachers and almost all the pupils. He broke into his own classroom and poured the petrol everywhere, over the floor and the furniture. On his way out he tossed the can and a lighter into the room and quickly closed the door. It was 10 o'clock.

Ken went across the road and waited. He could see the flames and smoke gathering force in the ground floor classroom and he remembers the sheer thrill of the windows bursting. His whole being was filled with incredible excitement and feelings of power. He had never experienced anything like it before. There was a tingling all over his body. It was almost sexual. Ken had not had sex before that night and only a small number of times subsequently. He always had a low sex drive and although he described himself as being heterosexual, most people who dealt with him felt he had little interest in sexual activity.

The flames were spreading to the next floor by the time the fire engines arrived. What a feeling. He had caused all of this. The noise, the flashing lights in the dark night, the movement and the confusion. He was in a daze but also sexually aroused. In a way, he was transfixed by the scene, consumed by the fire as if he were a part of it. Every cell in his body exulted. He was still in this euphoric state when the police took him away. Ken had not expected the fire to affect him so much. He admitted the offence and was given a three-year sentence in a youth custody institution.

In custody Ken had an unremarkable time. From time to time he was bullied but otherwise he remained mostly by himself. He missed the outside but did not miss his family much. When he was released he returned to his mother's house but failed to establish a good relationship with her.

He managed to get a job in a store and kept himself to himself. He started to drink a little and sometimes he got drunk. A number of small fires were noticed in the local vicinity, mostly on waste ground. These were not serious and it was assumed locally that they were caused by teenagers having cider parties.

At work the foreman reprimanded Ken for being lazy. Ken *was* quite lazy and avoided work from an early age. He was sometimes ridiculed for being so quiet and people also teased him about his sexuality. He hated this type of unpleasantness, especially because it often took place in front of the female employees. Ken quite liked one of the young women because she used to talk to him. Being made fun of in front of her made him very angry indeed. However, he lacked the confidence to stand up to his workmates and so the anger just festered inside. He decided he was going to get even with them all in the way he knew best.

One weekend Ken had several pints of beer. Once again he got a can of petrol. He broke into the factory where he worked, poured the petrol everywhere, over furniture and equipment, and threw the can and a lighter on to the petrol as he closed the door. As he walked away he felt the same exhilaration that he had experienced during his previous big fire, the one at the school. The fires on the waste ground and similar places were fine but nothing compared to this grand display. He could not resist going across the road to witness his handiwork and see all the commotion and the action with fire engines. He noticed himself becoming sexually aroused and he ejaculated. He felt very pleased that all his tormentors would be out of a job and that the bosses would be sorry.

At a later point it became important to Ken that they knew he was responsible. He was proud that he had got even with them all. He had no remorse for what he had done and he had never thought about the possibility of anyone being injured during the fire. There were often one or two security men on the premises and sometimes a few people working late. Ken would have known about this but it never entered his head. If he had thought about that it would not have bothered him. If someone was injured it would only have made things worse for the bosses and that would have pleased him.

He caused £50,000 worth of damage that night. He was sentenced to a maximum security hospital because it was decided in court that he had a serious personality disorder and was a danger to the public. Ken spent ten years at the security hospital mostly keeping to himself as he had done in custody earlier on. He was released because it was decided that he exhibited no signs of formal mental illness such as schizophrenia or depression. He never had any signs of those illnesses from the beginning. There was very little change in him in any way. He had been compliant during his time at the hospital and he seemed to respond to the close supervision and the ordered lifestyle of the institution.

People like Ken quite like things being organised for them and they often make ideal, trouble-free, inmates. They comply with all the rules and do what they are asked to do. This kind of lifestyle is relatively stress free for some people who find ordinary life on the outside difficult to cope with or to fit into. Sometimes, in the past, this compliance was taken as a sign of rehabilitation and some dangerous people were unwisely released – with unfortunate results. Specialists now recognise that this compliance in an institutional setting is not always a good indication of how serious offenders will behave on the outside.

Ken moved into a hostel with other former offenders. He seemed mild-mannered and tended to keep himself to himself. He liked to have a few pints of beer and sometimes he drank to excess. The hostel staff were often wary and a little afraid of Ken but they felt they were being unreasonable. They knew his history so they kept a close eye on him for the first few months. However, he settled in well initially and caused no problems. As time went on Ken had minor arguments with other residents but the staff never took sides. On several occasions Ken seemed unhappy and resentful about various issues such as whose turn it was to do the washing up or who had the right to choose the television programmes. Sometimes he said things like 'I'll get even with the lot of you,' but he did no more about it. The staff often felt uneasy when he spoke like this.

Many hostels and other residential establishments refuse to take arsonists under any conditions, even if they have been trouble free for a very long time. One can understand their reservations. The fear of the arsonist repeating his crime is very strong in many people's minds. He or she might set their next fire in the middle of the night and people could be burnt to death while they sleep.

Ken's case is a common type of arson story where the apparently quiet and inoffensive person can commit very destructive and violent offences and their motivation is not clear to the normal person. They are often quite angry inside and resentful towards different people such as previous teachers or employers. Sometimes these feelings are directed at society in general rather than any specific target. They may see others as having received a greater share of life's privileges and a better start in life than they did. This means that in some cases the act of arson can be seen as a gesture against a person or a class of people that the offender feels has treated him badly in some way. This kind of motivation may not be well formulated at the time of the offence and the arsonist may simply be feeling angry. He may decide to take action but the place to be set on fire may not be very carefully chosen. Alcohol may also play a part.

Around 50 per cent of arsonists have a serious alcohol problem and the offence occurs when they are intoxicated. Alcohol probably acts as a disinhibiting factor, as it does in many offences. When intoxicated the arsonist may get enough courage or alternatively sufficiently lose control over his behaviour to give in to his drives and act out his fantasies. While they are intoxicated, many offenders find that they can give themselves a licence to do what they really wanted to do anyway.

There are cases where a person causes fires accidentally while drunk and such a person may be charged with arson. This in understandable if it happens once or twice but some people come back many times with the same story so that one assumes that the fire-setting is a tendency in the person's personality that comes more to the surface with the effects of alcohol. One also comes across pranks that go wrong. The offenders may be drunk or otherwise intoxicated with substances such as ecstasy. These offences are not common because even while intoxicated, people treat fire with respect because of its massive potential for destruction.

Another 50 per cent of arsonists are mentally handicapped but there is considerable overlap with the 50 per cent who are alcoholics. Like most arsonists, the mentally handicapped arsonist gets a liking for fire at an early age. He learns which is the best time to set a fire and avoid detection. Playing with fire can be a game for some mentally handicapped people and they may enjoy striking matches and watching them burn out. A proportion then go further and set small fires either in their own homes or in the institution where they live or spend the day. In moderately handicapped individuals this activity is similar to the destructive acts of a child who is not fully aware of what he is doing. He may think it is funny and cannot understand why everyone is so upset about the result. For the mildly mentally handicapped person, the fire setting may be used more as a weapon and a means at getting back at people or institutions.

Why do arsonists commit their offences? The ordinary person often finds this type of crime hard to understand. As with many crimes there is a drive to commit the offence and to get away with it. There follows the urge to be found out, get publicity for one's handiwork and be famous. To the average person, a large fire can be exciting and we know that most people enjoy bonfires. However, setting a fire that will destroy a large amount of property and may endanger life is a different matter. Some arsonists say they just like to see the flames and hear the noise. The scene of a large fire is very exciting with sparkling and crackling flames. The noise of fire engines and firemen running around and shouting adds to this. There is also a strong feeling of danger as timbers and even walls groan, strain and crash to the ground. Others will admit to the powerful feelings they experience when they see the destructive power they have unleashed. They can set the whole process in motion with very little effort and destroy a whole building or property in a very short time.

Some arsonists get sexual stimulation and excitement from their fire and they may masturbate while watching the spectacle. These individuals sometimes admit to having erotic dreams which involve fires and flames.

A small number of arsonists say that their motivation is related to their love of fire engines. These offenders set the fire and wait for the engines and firemen to arrive. Some of these even help the firemen with their hoses and equipment. They may be the person who calls the fire service to make sure they get the type of show they want. This seems laughable especially because some of them fantasise that they are the hero of the scene when in fact they caused the fire in the first place. It is similar to the common boyish interest in trains and fire engines and sirens. The difference here is that the childish games and fantasies are allowed to become real. Such offenders are usually of low intelligence.

A common target for the younger arson offender, like Ken, is his own school. A teenager may perceive himself as a failure and blame the school for part of his inability to achieve academically or to be accepted and fit in with his peers. The teachers or one particular teacher may be the focus of the hatred, or the pupils in general. The young person's own classroom may be the first target and the fire may engulf and destroy the whole school. The school is only one of the typical arson targets.

In the rural setting the arsonist has always been especially feared, given the tendency for the fire-setter to repeat his crime. Loss of a haybarn and the contents is a real worry, as is the possible damage to livestock. Sometimes grudges are settled by this type of crime but the offender may cause more damage and destruction than he originally intended. People may be killed or badly injured because the offender was angry over something trivial.

Not all arsonists are male. Female arsonists are an interesting group. They frequently set fires near their own homes, in contrast to the male who usually chooses some site away from where he lives. The younger male arsonist may burn down his school but later on he often sets fires in locations away from his own neighbourhood. Some female arsonists set fire to their own rooms and thereby to the houses where they live. In a proportion of these cases the victim of the action is a spouse or her parents. The arsonist may feel wronged in some way by the person and wants to cause as much embarrassment, unpleasantness and financial loss as possible.

One such woman was Ann. She was in her early twenties and still lived at home. Her older brother and sister lived away from home but she never seemed to want to leave the nest. She never held a job for more than a few weeks either because she was fired or because she felt the job was not interesting enough. At school she performed poorly and she was noted as being a quiet, withdrawn girl who did not mix very well. She spent most of the time at home in her own room with her television. If she went out it was usually to buy alcohol or cigarettes.

Ann usually interacted with her parents only to demand money or other services from them. They were finding the situation more and more difficult to cope with as the years went by and things seemed to be getting worse rather than better. On one occasion she set a fire in a wastepaper basket following an argument with her parents. It caused minimal damage but frightened her parents and the rest of the family. The same thing happened several weeks later while she was drunk. On another occasion she threatened that she would kill herself if they did not give her money.

The last straw for the family was when she set a fire in her own room one night. This happened after the usual row concerning the money she extorted weekly from her parents. She stormed off to her room and the parents thought no more about it. However, about an hour later they smelled something burning and the father ran up the stairs to investigate. He was greeted with smoke billowing from under the door of Ann's room. They called the fire brigade and the father managed to pull his unconscious and drunk daughter from the flames and smoke.

The room was completely destroyed and so was part of the ceiling and the roof. The whole house could have easily been burned down and the three of them could have died. Ann was treated for smoke inhalation in the local general hospital for a week and then transferred to the local psychiatric hospital. No evidence of mental illness was found but she was kept as an in-patient for several weeks for assessment. It was recognised that she had self-destructive impulses and she clearly had the potential to set fires and harm others. The doctors made a diagnosis of a personality disorder. She was also addicted to alcohol and she needed some detoxification for this.

Ann's parents visited her and were very concerned but they refused to allow her live at home again. They were afraid she would cause their deaths. She was eventually moved to a group home where she lives with other people who are unable to cope in normal society.

Other people burn their own houses for various reasons. In some areas if a family wants a change of house and the council or local housing authority will not agree to it, burning one's house is a recognised way of forcing the situation. Arson is not easy to prove and so the housing authority can be in a difficult position. An unusual example of this type of crime involved a family from a working class area in a large city. The man was un-employed and the couple often drank heavily. They had three children ranging in age from about one to ten years of age. On two occasions in the past their house had been damaged by fire. The first time was thought to be part of a drunken episode and several rooms in the house were destroyed. About a year later the family asked to be moved from the second house but the council refused. Soon afterwards the house was seriously damaged by fire, again to such an extent that the family had to be moved. There was no proof of any illegal action by the couple at that time.

Approximately two years later another fire took place. The house was burnt out completely. The mother and two of the children were killed. The eldest son escaped by climbing out an upstairs window and jumping from a ledge. He was unhurt. The father appeared on the scene and watched from the other side of the road. He was upset as the three bodies were brought out and pleased to see that one of the children had survived. The police, however, thought that his level of distress was less than they would have expected, and they very soon became suspicious. They investigated his movements and his version of what might have happened and subsequently arrested him. He was charged with murder and eventually went to trial. His explanation was that the fire was set to force the council to move the family again. This was not accepted by the court as it was shown that he had deliberately set the fire while the rest of the family were asleep upstairs. He was found guilty of murder and sentenced to life imprisonment. It was never very clear why he killed his wife and children.

Are some arsonists mentally ill? In general they are not, but a proportion may have strange personalities. A small proportion are suffering from a mental illness such as schizophrenia. James had a long history of contact with his local psychiatric service. He had a diagnosis of schizophrenia and had had persecutory delusions and hallucinations over many years. He killed a woman one night in an old house in response to hallucinatory voices. The voices told him that she was the devil and that he must kill her to save others. He set fire to the house and it was completely burnt down. He survived the fire and was eventually found guilty but insane. It was established at his trial that he did not know what he was doing at the time of the killing because of his mental illness. The judge committed him to a maximum security psychiatric institution.

Sometimes one sees a schizophrenic person charged with arson after he sets a fire in a derelict house. In order to keep warm he may have been setting a small fire which got out of hand. The correct course for the authorities in many of these of cases is to have the person properly connected with his local psychiatric service. This may mean initially committing the person to a psychiatric hospital. Occasionally, a mentally ill person may burn down a house, typically his own house, because he believes the devil is in the house and he must be exorcised from it. This is very rare but it may happen that burning the house can result in an unintentional homicide.

When a mentally ill person commits a serious offence such as arson, especially where someone is killed, the occurrence is usually widely reported in the media. This type of story is easily remembered by the general public and in many people's minds it strengthens the idea that the mentally ill person is unpredictable and dangerous.

This stereotype is inaccurate and very unfair to people with mental illnesses. People with mental illnesses are no more likely to be dangerous than other members of the general public. If they do act dangerously it is much more likely to be against themselves, for instance by committing suicide.

When an individual is charged in connection with an arson offence the charge is usually one of criminal damage to property or criminal damage by fire. If the fire 'accidentally' kills another person they did not know was in the house they are usually charged with attempted murder as well. This is because it is assumed that they were 'reckless' as to whether another person was in danger in the building, in not checking that the building was empty and that no one was at risk.

Sometimes a person who is suffering from a serious depression or some other psychiatric illness takes his or her own life with fire. It is not a common method of suicide. Joseph was a middle-aged man with a grown up family. He had suffered from a chronic depressive disorder for several years and had to resign from his job. He had depression episodes lasting several months at a time and these were very distressing to himself and others around him. One day after lunch, without warning, he went out into the garden shed, poured petrol over himself, set it alight and killed himself. There was no prior indication that he had any suicidal intent and the family reported that he seemed in slightly brighter spirits that morning than he had been for weeks. The suicide was naturally very traumatic for his family and for others who had cared from him.

Insurance fraud is a common criminal type of fire setting so insurance companies investigate fires where there is a large claim and any suspicious features. There is no psychiatric aberration but simply an attempt to obtain money illegally. Sometimes the owner of a failing company that is in debt sees arson as way out of a hopeless situation. Such offenders sometimes serve long prison sentences. Sometimes they commit their offences while drunk but they usually know fully what they are doing.

What can be done for arsonists? The answer to this question depends on what is wrong with them in the first place. If the person is mentally ill, with a problem such as schizophrenia or manic depression, he or she needs to be treated properly by the local psychiatric service. If alcohol abuse is an important contributor to the problem then this needs addressing with the help of Alcoholics Anonymous or other agencies. However, getting people with alcohol problems to stop drinking is not easy, as everyone knows. If the individual's problem is a mental handicap, he or she may need ongoing close supervision either in the person's own home, if that is where he or she lives, or in an institution. Many arsonists have personality problems which are not easily treated. Some may need to spend time in security hospitals or prisons for the protection of the public. The hopeful news is that the majority of arsonists seem to stop committing this offence when they get into their late twenties and early thirties.

5
FEMALE OFFENDERS

Crime seems to be mostly a male activity; only about 5 per cent of criminal convictions involve females. Violent crime is almost exclusively a male activity and sexual crime is even more male dominated. The tiny number of females in our prison systems is further evidence of this huge sex difference. Among psychiatric patients there is no such difference and in some surveys females slightly outnumber males in psychiatric hospitals and registers. This means that the crime difference is probably not related to psychiatric issues.

However, women are represented, if only in small numbers, in all categories of crime and there are some categories of crime where females are in the majority: shoplifting, certain types of child abduction and prostitution. Men are represented in these categories too but females have always remained in the majority. In the case of shoplifting, the female preponderance is diminishing all the time, as more and more young men are convicted of this offence, and male conviction rates are now very near the female level. Traditionally, the male shoplifter and the female have stolen different types of goods. He tended to steal hardware and books while the woman tended to take clothes. Both usually took goods in order to convert them into money for drugs or alcohol or for no particular reason. Young men are now more likely than before to be convicted for taking clothes. However, the male equivalent of the depressed middle-aged female shoplifter does not yet appear to have evolved.

CHILD ABDUCTION

Child abduction causes enormous distress to parents. When a child is taken, whether it is a newborn infant or a three-year-old, the parents go through extreme torment and fear. They feel guilty that they were unable to protect the child and immediately assume that the worst possible things have happened, that the child has been murdered, probably after being tortured or abused. They worry in case the child has been abandoned and is dying alone at that very moment or that he or she has been stolen by a mad person and is going to have a short life of torment and suffering. Or that the child has been sold into some adoption ring either in the home country or internationally, or a sexual abuse ring.

Abductions take place in different situations. The commonest cases one sees nowadays are where one spouse decides to remove his or her child from one country, such as Ireland, to another country, such as the UK. This is the only type of abduction where men are more common offenders but both men and women can be involved, and the traffic can go in either direction. It is nearly always in the context of a disharmonious marital separation. There is a dispute about rights over the children and the aggrieved party decides to take the law into his or her own hands. The child is seldom harmed as the abductor is usually a caring but unhappy parent. The other parent has a distressing time as he or she waits for news about the abducted child or children. These disputes can become very unpleasant if the couple who split up are playing this drama out on a wider international stage, say between Iraq and the UK. Nobody wins in these situations. The High Court in Ireland deals with abduction cases and always puts them top of the agenda of the court's business when they arise. The guiding principle is that the ruling of the original court that determined custody or access is upheld, unless some very unusual circumstance has intervened. The matter is usually referred back to the original court for it to deal with it.

A different form of child stealing or child abduction are considered to be predominantly female crimes. A woman has given birth to a baby who was either stillborn or died soon after birth. Subsequent to this, she becomes mentally ill with a severe postnatal depression or the less common puerperal psychosis. In this state the woman may believe that some other child, such as a child she may encounter in a hospital or in the street, is really her baby. This delusion is part of her mental illness. She also believes that her own baby did not die and that it was all a mistake or even a conspiracy against her. The woman takes the baby from the cot in the maternity hospital or from the pram in the street and brings him or her home.

The infant is nearly always located in a few days. When the woman's family realise what has happened they get in touch with the authorities and the child is returned to the parents. This process can take a little longer if the woman who steals the child is a single mother living alone. The woman is normally not charged with any offence because it is usually obvious that she is mentally ill. She is put into the care of her local psychiatric services for treatment. The real mother and father will have gone through days of absolute hell from which it may take them a long time to recover. Such children are normally not in the least harmed as the mentally ill woman who abducts the infant believes that she is the mother and that the child is her own. Consequently, she loves the child as a mother and takes good care of him or her.

In a similar scenario a woman with a personality disorder and low intelligence steals a child because she believes her marriage depends on her having a baby. Such a woman is usually not mentally ill but very immature and unable to understand the enormity of her actions. She may have a history of losing a baby, such as a late miscarriage or a stillbirth. She may believe that she is pregnant or she may really want to be. Her husband, who may also be of low intelligence, is taken in by her fantasy and believes her when she says they will soon have a baby. She may then leave him for a few days and return with an infant whom she has stolen from a maternity hospital or elsewhere. The husband simply accepts that the new baby is theirs and life goes on in their household. The child is well cared for as the woman acts as any mother would. The man believes he is the father as he has no reason to suspect anything is wrong. If such children are not found by the authorities within a short time they may never be found. Fortunately for parents, such cases are very uncommon.

There seems to be a small but real international business which involves children being stolen and sold on for adoption and perhaps even sexual abuse. This is a real fear in areas of the US and other countries as far away as South Africa. The perpetrators here may be males or females or teams of both.

Prostitution

This is almost exclusively a female crime and has been with us since the beginnings of civilisation. It is often seen as a form of continuous abuse of women by men. The pimp is one of the abusers and the customer who allows the institution to stay in existence is the other. In films and books we are often presented with a glamorised picture of this profession in the form of the beautiful and exclusive callgirl or the Cinderella tale. The reality of prostitution on the streets or brothels in cities around the world is much seedier and more unpleasant.

In Ireland the offence of soliciting has been very rarely prosecuted in recent years. In 1993 there was one conviction; in 1994 thirteen. The current practice of the gardai is to encourage prostitutes to move on so that they will not cause a nuisance in any one area. Very occasionally, people are convicted of living on the earnings of prostitutes, for instance running a brothel. There have been suggestions that men who use prostitutes should be charged with offences such as loitering, but prosecutions of this sort are extremely rare.

Many prostitutes have a history of abuse which may include child sexual abuse and neglect. This abuse often continues into their adult lives in the relationship with the pimp. Some may be married to their pimp and others may be one of a number of women controlled by this man. Such men dominate these women by violence, very effectively in most cases.

Prostitutes also face violence from their customers on a daily basis. Some men engage prostitutes for sex, then feel free to beat them up, afterwards justifying their actions on the grounds that she was 'only a prostitute'. Or a prostitute may decline to have sex with a man, perhaps because she is afraid of him, and he rapes her. In recent years there have been convictions for rape and sexual assault of prostitutes. Every year a number of prostitutes are murdered and there are always stories of serial killers who target prostitutes.

Many prostitutes have problems with substance abuse. The commonest problem is, as usual, alcohol, and because many of them attract their custom in pubs, their customers as a consequence are often intoxicated. This makes violence more likely. Intoxicated men often have difficulties sustaining an erection and even if they get an erection, they have problems ejaculating. Some men blame the woman for this failing. The other prevalent substance problem among prostitutes is heroin addiction, often the reason women become engaged in prostitution in the first place. Their lives become a nightmare spiral of prostitution and drug abuse.

Prostitutes are particularly prone to disease. Women who have an intravenous heroin problem may well contract HIV. The number of sexual contacts these women have also greatly increase their chances of contracting HIV. The old sexually transmitted diseases, such as syphilis and gonorrhoea, are still there, and there are the newer problems of Hepatitis B and C.

Some community care services, such as the Eastern Health Board in Dublin, have targeted prostitutes and provide special clinics for them where they have continuity of care. They are encouraged to have regular health checks and blood tests, a very beneficial arrangement.

A small proportion of prostitutes suffer from mental illness such as schizophrenia, and some are mentally handicapped. These need to be referred to local psychiatric or mental handicap services when they are picked up by professional agencies. Of course, many of these may not be picked up, or if they are, they may not comply with the services or treatments.

HOMICIDE AND WOMEN

The vast majority of homicides are committed by men; in only about 5 per cent of homicides the perpetrator is a woman. A common homicide scenario would involve a woman who has been repeatedly beaten and abused by her husband or partner, frequently an alcoholic. The woman is totally demoralised and traumatised by this torment. Finally she explodes with pent-up anger and frustration. She may stab her partner as he attacks her or she may hit him on the head with some heavy object, such as a hammer, as he sleeps in front of the television. It may be an act solely of self defence because she believes the assaulting man is going to kill or seriously injure her during a prolonged violent attack.

A similar psychological mechanism which is mentioned on occasion in murder trials is the 'over-controlled personality'. The woman absorbs many insults and traumas over a very long time and appears to be coping reasonably well. She may seem tense to the onlooker but not noticeably abnormal. Then she is subjected to one last assault, not necessarily the most severe, which breaks the camel's back. Her reaction is catastrophic and she kills the persecutor. Such a killing may be frenzied; instead of one or two stab wounds there may be twenty. It is as if, once the volcano erupts, there is no controlling the consequences.

Women who kill their abusing husbands are doubly traumatised. They may have been battered and abused, perhaps for years, and now have the added burden of the killing. The courts usually treat these women sympathetically and some are acquitted on the grounds of self defence. Others are found guilty of manslaughter and given short prison sentences or even probation. Occasionally such cases go against the women and they are found guilty of murder. The jury decides that they fully intended to kill the men and that they were responsible for their actions at the time. The judge has no option but to sentence such defendants to life imprisonment but some of them succeed in having the charge reduced to manslaughter on appeal. Even if they are not successful in their appeal, they tend to spend a much shorter time in prison on the life sentence that the standard murderer.

An interesting female homicide case occurred in the mid-1980s in the UK. Anne was eighteen years of age. She was a very bright girl and always wanted to be a writer or a journalist. Her father had died when she was eleven. She missed him a great deal and her childhood was unhappy because she felt isolated and lonely. She had a relationship with an older man and became pregnant. She concealed this pregnancy from everyone, including her mother. Privately, she arranged to have the child adopted but parting from the child caused her great suffering and pain. She developed a postnatal depressive disorder but she tried to get back to a normal way of living by overworking. Her relationship with her mother deteriorated greatly and her constant nagging was more than Anne could withstand. One night, in a haze of mental disorder combined with anguish at the loss of her baby and her inability to cope with her mother, she killed her with a hammer.

Following a traumatic time on remand in HMP Holloway Anne went for trial. Despite clear evidence that she was mentally ill at the time of the killing, the jury convicted her of murder and she was sentenced to life imprisonment. This result shocked all who were involved in the case, and her plight became the focus for many sympathisers. On appeal, the court accepted new evidence relating to pre-menstrual syndrome and Anne's likely hormonal state at the time of the killing in the light of her recent pregnancy. This, combined with the previous diagnosis of postnatal depression, persuaded the court to reduce the conviction to manslaughter. She was released from prison on a two-year probation order. Anne's fascinating story is told in her own book called *Tightrope, the Autobiography of Anne Reynolds* (Sidgwick & Jackson, 1990).

SHOPLIFTERS
Maria was fifty-five and lived in a small town near a large city. She and her husband had three grown-up children. Her husband had a good job locally and was well known.

They had grown apart over about five years and her husband became more interested in his work than in the home. In frequent arguments they both said hurtful things, then hardly spoke to each other for days on end. Their children tended to stay out of the house as much as possible and tried not to side with either parent.

Maria became increasingly frustrated and unhappy with her life. Her husband stayed at work until very late in the evening and she suspected that he was having an affair with a colleague. Her own family lived hundreds of miles away but they had never been very close anyway. In the evenings she was often alone. She started taking sedative medication which was prescribed by one doctor and eventually by several. She became quite skilful at manipulating these medical advisers.

Maria's alcohol consumption increased to the extent that she was drinking half a bottle of vodka several days per week. She thought nobody noticed. The children did but they felt powerless. She became increasingly isolated and was frequently depressed and weepy, especially when alone at night.

Things became so bad that she felt she could not stand it in the house any more so she moved into a flat in the same town. None of the family objected as they increasingly regarded her as an alcoholic, a burden and as an embarrassment. The children could never bring friends home because they could not be sure what condition she would be in. She refused to go for any form of help or counselling when her husband or the children tried to arrange it.

One day Maria was wandering in a large clothes shop

when she got an urge to put some packets of stockings into her bag. She had drunk some vodka earlier in the day and was feeling a little fuzzy mentally from the alcohol and the effects of her early morning sedatives. This urge persisted and she gave in to it. She put the packets into her bag and walked out of the shop although she did not need them and had plenty of money in her purse.

Once out of the shop she felt confused and a little guilty but also exhilarated. Several times a week she did the same thing in different shops. A few months later she became careless. Usually she would check where the security person was but eventually she started not to care. Her mood continued to fluctuate and her abuse of alcohol and sedative medication continued so that the shoplifting was often done in a fog of intoxication. Then she was caught.

She was discharged from court but she was back before the court again the following week. She was given probation but this did not change her behaviour. Every day she was getting caught, almost on purpose, and eventually the court had to give her a short sentence, and then a longer one.

During her time in prison she was put in contact with the psychiatric service and she maintained this contact as an outpatient with her local psychiatric service. They were able to help her get her sedative drug and alcohol abuse under control, then her other problems. She was very slow to change and slow to understand her behaviour or to take responsibility for her actions. It also took her a long time to come to terms with the break-up of her marriage.

Eventually she was able to rebuild her relationship with

her children. She started to examine her motivation for the shoplifting, which was often associated with a rising urge to steal the goods and the feeling of exhilaration which followed. She felt in control in some way at those times, as if she had got one over on the security people, the store and the whole 'system'. The danger of being nearly caught heightened the experience. Later, actually being caught was the most satisfying part because the local papers always carried the stories. This caused great embarrassment to the well known husband whom she had grown to despise. He was the real victim of her criminal behaviour and in the later period he was her main target. Causing him unhappiness seemed to justify her behaviour. In about 5 to 10 per cent of shoplifting cases where the offender is female, the histories would be similar to Maria's. The offenders are middle-aged women who may have marriage problems and depressive symptoms to varying extents. Some have a history of being beaten by their husbands and in other cases the partner may be having an affair. They frequently have alcohol and sedative drug abuse problems as well. It is often difficult to know if the substance abuse problems came before the marriage and depressive problems or the other way around. These shoplifters tend to steal things that they do not want or need and they usually have sufficient money in their pockets to pay. Their motive is very rarely money, as is the case with ordinary shoplifters.

Most of these women respond reasonably well to counselling. A smaller number may need anti-depressant medication for a period if their main problem is a clinical depression. Marital or family therapy may also be useful if the parties involved are willing and motivated. Other couples may need mediation and help with the break-up of the relationship and the separation. The substance abuse, which is common in these cases, may need attention in its own right and in such cases it needs to be tackled before any other useful work can be done.

Sometimes one comes across interesting variants of Maria's case where the woman has a history of unhappiness in her relationships and in her family. Here the offender may only be happy stealing jewellery or expensive clothes. The woman is responding to her unhappy domestic situation in the same way as Maria but she may have certain high standards below which she cannot sink.

Foreign students and sometimes foreign wives may belong to an unusual category of shoplifters. Foreign students sometimes take goods from shops, seeming to feel that it is a very minor affair. They cannot understand why the police are involved and why they are being charged before a court. Their offence causes all kinds of difficulties for their host family or organisation, not to mention their own family back home. The foreign wife who shoplifts, for example the wife of a diplomat or a business-man, also causes great concern and embarrassment. She may be in an unhappy marriage, feeling isolated in what is to her a foreign country. Her actions may be a cry for help, or intended to cause difficulties for what she perceives as an uncaring or unsupportive husband, as in Maria's case.

Kleptomania is a term that the general public still associate with this type of offending but psychiatrists reserve this term for a rare obsessive-compulsive type of disorder where the person has a recurring, mounting urge to steal from shops. The urge to steal causes an irresistible excitement which is relieved only by the stealing. The person may describe a feeling of detachment, as if in a dream, or they may say that they felt an almost euphoric glow over their bodies.

Approximately 5 per cent of shoplifters are mentally ill with disorders such as schizophrenia. They may steal food because they are homeless, hungry and unable to look after themselves. These are always sad cases. The choice of goods stolen is often inappropriate or irrational as the following case illustrates:

Patrick was in his mid twenties. He was single and had lost all contact with his family, who came from a country area and increasingly found Patrick's behaviour difficult to cope with. He constantly paced around his room at night talking to hallucinatory voices. From time to time he was treated in his local psychiatric hospital but when he was out of the hospital's care he relapsed because he stopped complying with treatment. He left his home and soon drifted to a large city where he stayed in hostels. Soon he stopped attending to personal hygiene and he lost all contact with his family and the services. He started living rough.

He was often hungry. One day he went into a supermarket and took a large uncooked ham and put it under his scruffy anorak. Then he put another ham under the anorak. What was he going to do with these? He had no way of cooking them. The theft was a totally irrational act. He tried to walk out of the shop like this and was cooperative when the bewildered check-out person asked him to wait until she called the manager. He made no attempt to run away. The manager called the police and Patrick was taken into custody and later committed to prison on remand. The court was advised that he was not a criminal but a sad and chronically mentally ill individual. The charges were dropped on condition that he be transferred to his local psychiatric hospital for treatment and supervised follow-up.

The majority of shoplifters are not mentally ill or trying to work out some traumatic situation in their present or past lives. They steal from shops, or anywhere else for that matter, because they want the goods themselves or they intend to sell the goods for money. Shoplifting has become so serious for large and small retailers internationally that it is estimated that 20 per cent of the retail price on goods is there to offset the cost of losses. This means that the cost of replacing goods, insurance, security personnel and security equipment such as cameras and alarms on doors is borne to a large extent by the customer.

Larger stores seem to suffer more from this problem. Offenders of this kind tend to have very little remorse about their offences, which they see as having no victims other than an impersonal chain store which is very rich or well insured. They do not see the victim in terms of the ordinary person in the street who is paying for their crimes because of the higher prices. If they did realise this it might still not make much difference to them.

To counteract the fact that many professional shop-lifters are well known in an area it is now common for groups of these offenders to hire minibuses to take them to other areas, pastures new for shoplifting. Many shop-lifters enjoy these trips and regard them as real social occasions. For some of these offenders shoplifting can be fun and they admit that they enjoy their profession.

The disposal of the goods acquired has also become very organised. This means that offenders have a ready network to sell on their goods quickly. The type of garments or other items that are required by this under-ground system may also be specified so the shoplifter knows what is needed. This phenomenon is also evident in house-breaking and burglary. Offenders may be given an order for a particular type of video, TV or even car radio.

The crimes men commit in shops are more likely to be 'jump overs' or hold-ups. Their target is cash and they get it by threatening the counter staff with objects such as hammers, knives and more frequently now, guns. Some shops seem to be targeted on a regular basis and those at particular risk seem to be those with other cash businesses on site such as post offices or Lottery outlets.

The vast majority of shoplifting offenders are not psychiatrically ill. However, in prison one sees a lot of heroin-addicted female offenders who finance their habit by shoplifting. In the UK some of these women seem to use a combination of prostitution and shoplifting, whereas in Ireland they rely mostly on shoplifting. Some addicts supplement their revenue from shoplifting with minor drug selling. They need to lay their hands on up to £200 per day to finance their addiction.

Many of this latter group will appear before court on many occasions so that there is no alternative but a prison sentence. They often live very unhappy lives with chaotic domestic situations. Their husbands or boyfriends are frequently heroin addicts as well and may also be dying from HIV. Some such women have been abused all through their lives, both physically and sexually. Some of those who are HIV positive feel that they have nothing to lose, do not see any point in trying to control their drugtaking or undergoing any form of rehabilitation or indeed in stopping offending. Some even see prison as a not too unpleasant break from their very unhappy existence; at least there they get proper nourishment and medical attention.

The role of the psychiatrist *vis-à-vis* shoplifting offenders depends on where he or she comes in contact with them. In the community he would try to identify psychiatric disturbance such as schizophrenia or depression, treat the disorder or refer the person to his or her local catchment area psychiatric service. If the problem is like Maria's, alcohol and sedative abuse combined with marital and mood problems, the approach will be to help her cope with at addictions first, then the relationship problems. For the heroin addict, who may or may not be HIV positive, the priority is to help them stabilise the drug addiction. A minority will try to stop drugtaking but others will opt for a maintenance programme using methadone, a heroin substitute. Social intervention by various agencies to help such people build up a reasonable lifestyle is not often successful but should always be explored.

Offenders who enjoy shoplifting are more difficult because they often believe that there is no problem. The criminal who decides to make money from crime seldom requires a psychiatrist to help him stop offending.

PART II
INSIDE THE MINDS OF VICTIMS

6
VICTIMS OF RAPE

A VIOLENT ASSAULT

Emma left the disco at around 2.00 am. It was a little later than she planned because she had delayed to talk to a girl she had not seen since secondary school. Emma was nineteen. She lived three miles away from the disco and her plan was to get a taxi home with her two work friends. Her parents knew that Emma was sensible and were happy that she and her friends had arranged to come home together. When she got to the door of the disco she realised that the other two had left without her. She could not get a taxi so she decided to walk alone the three miles through the built-up city area. It was an area she knew very well. Most of the journey was along a main road then there was a short section by her old school and finally a walk through some housing estates. She had drunk very little, one bottle of lager, so she was sober and alert.

There were no problems until she started to walk by the old school. She noticed two young men drinking what appeared to be cans of beer inside the gates. She took no notice and continued walking. There was no one else around. This was the most deserted part of the route but she knew she was almost half-way home now. As she was coming near the end of the low school wall she heard fast walking feet behind her.

She glanced around as her heart quickened. At that point one of the men grabbed her around the neck and pulled her over the wall. She was dazed and shocked. At first she struggled to get free but then she became frozen with fear. It was as if she were in a trance, looking on from the outside. Both men dragged her to a place behind the school buildings.

At that point she recovered some strength and realised she was being attacked and would probably be raped or even killed. She was terrified. She started to scream and struggle as strongly as she could. One of the men shouted at her and started punching her in the face and body. She became dazed again, almost immobilised by fright.

Both men raped her then, each in turn while she was held down by the other. There was hardly any need to hold her down because she was unable to resist. One of them punched her again and insisted on oral sex. Both assailants were about her own age but she did not recognise them. Both were intoxicated and laughed and giggled a lot in between shouting at her, which suggests that they may have been intoxicated with other substances as well as with alcohol. They both kicked and punched her again before they left her in the schoolyard.

Emma recovered somewhat after about twenty minutes and struggled home. When she got there she was crying and shaking so much it was difficult for her parents to understand what had happened. She was bleeding from the punches to her face and the sexual attack. Her parents phoned the police and went around to the local station.

The police were very kind. A female police officer handled most of the police business with Emma and did everything to comfort her and support her. But it seemed to her that the questions would never end. She could not remember exactly what happened and she could not give a clear description of the assailants. It was like trying to remember a nightmare when most of your mind is trying to block out any memory of it. The police doctor came later and Emma was examined all over by her. She was also kind but Emma had never been examined like this by a doctor she had never met before. It was all so distressing and painful, especially when she had done nothing wrong? Swabs were taken from every orifice and also intimate hair clippings. Emma did not really understand what was going on and it all added to her sense of being out of control and violated.

Emma made a statement to the police and was interviewed by them on numerous occasions over the next week. She was asked to give further descriptions of the men and encouraged to look at police photographs but was not able to add much to her original account.

From the time of the rape Emma felt dirty inside and out. Her body had been invaded in the most horrible way and she had to get clean again. She washed, showered and bathed on many occasions in the first few days but it made no difference. Twelve months later that feeling of being dirty had not fully gone away.

She felt empty and numb inside for weeks. It was as if some part of her person or her humanity had been taken away and nothing was left in its place. She was unable to concentrate on anything and found herself crying for no reason. She found it difficult to get to sleep but if she did she would be woken up by terrifying nightmares. These were often related to the incident; she would see horrible images and heads where the perpetrators' heads had been. She often woke up terrified, sweating and shaking.

During the day things were also very difficult. Emma became very withdrawn. When her friends called to see her she told her mother to say she was sick in bed with a headache. After a month or two they stopped calling. Three weeks after the incident she tried to go back to work in the office where she was a typist. She could not do a thing at work and her boss drove her home half-way through the morning. Twelve months later she decided to try to get back to work initially for a few hours a day. The firm she worked for was very supportive.

Emma found it extremely difficult to go outside the house, especially at night, so she spent all her time at home with her parents. It was distressing for them too. One very good friend continued to visit and she was able to encourage her to go shopping and walking. It was only after a year that she could be persuaded to go for a drink with this friend in the evening.

From time to time a police officer still called round to see how she was. Her recovery was going to take a long time. The assailants were never caught.

The recovery period for rape victims varies enormously. Emma's difficulty in returning to a normal level of functioning is quite common, a proportion of cases even worse. Most victims who come forward have symptoms similar to Emma's during the first year or so after a serious sexual assault. Some seem on the surface to have recovered but the psychological scarring may disable them in a subtle way to the extent that they may never be able to reach their full potential as a human being.

FACTORS IN RECOVERY

There is a number of factors that have an influence on the rate of recovery for victims. One is the severity of the assault itself. If the assault was very brutal and violent it is more likely to have a lasting effect on the person, for instance if the victim is very seriously beaten over a long period. Occasionally, victims of rape suffer serious or permanent injuries such as broken bones or even the loss of a limb or an eye. It has been suggested that some rapists purposely injure victims' eyes in order that they will not be able to identify them. I have not come across this phenomenon myself so I assume it is quite rare.

In another small proportion of rape cases the victim is killed. This of course is the extreme expression of violence against the person. Most of these killings seem to be part of the general violence against the victim at the time. In some it may be the cold-blooded action of the ruthless sex assailant in order to avoid detection.

Alcohol is involved in the majority of rape and seriously sexual assaults. Approximately 60 per cent of the attackers are intoxicated with alcohol at the time of the attack and, interestingly, approximately 30 per cent of victims. This is more commonly seen where the two were drinking together beforehand and the situation turned into an assault later. We see more sexual assaults now where the assailant is intoxicated with other substances as well as alcohol, such as marijuana, sedative medication and Ecstasy.

THE ATTACK

What happens during the assault itself also affects the rate of recovery. Sometimes rape is single acts by an assailant and the whole episode is over in a relatively short time, like half an hour. Such a relatively brief assault may occur in situations where the victim knows the assailant, as in a date rape, even in the case of an attack by a stranger in a park at night. Other attacks can go on for hours and involve repeated sexual assaults. Clearly, the more prolonged the attack the worse it is for the victim in terms of the eventual physical and mental outcome. In a proportion of rapes the victim is forced to perform oral sex on the assailant and this is often very traumatic for the terrified woman. If the assailant fails to ejaculate during such oral sex, which is often the case, he can become more violent to the woman because he blames this on her. The drunken rapist who cannot sustain his erection is an added danger. He may get angry at the woman, blame her for his problem and as a result beat her more. In some cases the sexual assaults may involve anal sex, painful and distressing. Assailants sometimes insert objects such as a tennis racquet handle or a brush handle to add to the distress of the victim. There seems to be no limit to the depravity of some rapists.

In many cases of sexual assault the woman reports feeling she was going to die. She would have grounds for such feelings because some sexual assaults do end in homicide either by accident, by mindless drunken violence or by design on the part of the rapist. Victims are threatened: 'if you scream, I'll kill you,' or 'if you move, I'll kill you.' This is one of the factors that numbs women into total submission. In many cases the woman is threatened directly with a weapon, such as a knife being held to her throat. Such incidents often have long-lasting effects on the victim as the reality of the nearness of her own death is indelibly imprinted on her mind.

Occasionally, one encounters the deliberate kidnapping and the use of young men or women or children for sexual purposes and torture. Here the victim very seldom survives. The sadistic sexual serial killer procures his victims, young adults or young children in the case of the paedophile, for sexual gratification. This usually involves planned and even ritualised torture and sexual abuse of the victim before he or she is killed.

When there is more than one assailant the woman is usually more traumatised by the experience. Some researchers suggest that in 20 per cent of rape cases there are multiple attackers. The violence can be worse in these cases, as two or more rapists egg each other on. One or more of the offenders may hold the victim down while another rapes her; both may be involved in the general violence.

Victims are often afraid of disease following a sexual assault and this adds to the trauma. It is important that appropriate swabs and blood tests are taken to rule out diseases such as gonorrhoea and syphilis. Of increasing concern is the chance of being infected with HIV and the individual needs to be tested for that repeatedly over a six to twelve-month period to make sure she is disease free.

Another fear of the rape victim is pregnancy. The actual incidence of this is small but it is a real fear. Rape victims need to have early pregnancy testing, it is hoped to rule out pregnancy. If a woman becomes pregnant as a result of the rape it presents her and her family with new dilemmas. Many people would say that this is one of the few situations where abortion is acceptable. Others would argue that even this pregnancy, one that started as a result of rape and sexual assault, should not be aborted, that because the child who has been conceived is guilty of no crime it should not be destroyed. I suppose the only way society can deal with this complex moral dilemma is to allow the woman to make up her own mind and be master of her own future. If she is strongly against abortion, the pregnancy will be a terrible extra traumatic burden for her.

In about one-third of rapes the victim and attacker know each other. The commonest occurrence is date rape but such a victim may be raped by a boyfriend's friend or a boyfriend of her own friend or some other family or social connection. Cases of rape in marriage only rarely come before the criminal courts. Histories of sexual abuse within marriage are much more likely to come before the family law courts in judicial separation or divorce proceedings and in nullity actions.

OLDER VICTIMS OF RAPE

Not all female rape victims are young women and children. A female of any age may be a victim of rape and sexual assault. Services are increasingly coming across cases where women in their sixties and seventies are attacked by burglars and intruders in their houses. Often such young men are intoxicated with alcohol or other drugs. If they find a woman, even an elderly woman, they may decide to sexually assault her. This is often a savage assault on a frail woman who may never get over the trauma. Some die at the time and some die later from various injuries. The psychological symptoms suffered by surviving victims can be extremely disabling.

Some offenders have histories of repeated physical and sexual attacks on elderly women. These are a rare breed but they do exist. The idea of raping an older woman excites them, and older woman are an easy target. Rape in this case may be combined with burglary.

Sexual abuse or rape may also be part of the phenomenon of 'elder abuse', which is being increasingly recognised internationally. In such a case, the offender may be a son who is unable to cope with the demands of being a carer and who may, in addition, have an alcohol problem.

The Victim's Personality

The personality of the victim is an important factor in determining the rate of her eventual recovery from the attack. Some people seem better able than others to deal with a trauma, put it all behind them and get on with the rest of their lives. On the other hand, they may merely appear to be coping. They may be more timid and afraid than before and be unable to take the risks that normal people take on a daily basis throughout their lives. Such women might be inclined to stay at home rather than go out with friends and be slow to risk making new friends, especially men. A long time later, even years later, they may be totally unable to deal with some crisis, an inability linked to the buried trauma of the earlier assault.

It must be said, however, that many assault victims do make a good and lasting recovery and this is a product of their personality make-up at the time. I say 'at the time' because one's ability to cope with stressful events in life varies. If a victim is under a lot of pressure at a particular time, for whatever reason, such as work difficulties, problems in her family or relationships, it is only reasonable to expect that she would cope less well with a sexual assault than she might at another stage in her life.

Other rape victims seem to fall apart directly after the attack and never fully get back to their previous level of functioning. All sexual attacks are serious but sometimes the attacks that seem to be on the less serious end of the spectrum produce the worse traumatic effects on the victim. The meaning of the outrage and violation for that particular victim is a very important issue. This combines with her ability to cope with stresses in life in general and her coping skills at that particular time in her life to produce an outcome which can be quite variable.

Support for the Victim

The level of support received by a victim following sexual assault is recognised as important in his or her eventual recovery and return to normality. The first point of contact may be the police and this should be positive and supportive. The garda in Ireland and police in the UK have responded by providing female officers and also some male officers who have special training in investigating sexual crime and in dealing with the victims. They understand that the person is a victim first and a witness second. Questioning is conducted in a supportive and sensitive manner. Female doctors, who are also experienced in supporting the victim, are there whenever possible to collect medical evidence, such as swabs and hair clippings.

The individual's own family is the main support group, and victims with caring and integrated family backgrounds tend to do better in the long term. In the case of the younger victim, if she has a reasonable relationship with her parents, they will comfort her and help her get over the trauma of the assault and to support her through other hurdles such as the ongoing police investigations and court hearings. The married woman who may have a family of her own needs the support and understanding of her husband and children, if they are old enough.

The next layer of support mechanisms for the victim comprises the family doctor, psychiatric, social work and psychological services and other agencies such as the rape crisis centres in Ireland and the UK. The staff of these centres probably see the largest number of victims and are usually very skilled at helping them to cope with what has happened. They are often overburdened with referrals because victims of sexual assault are more likely now to come forward and report what has happened to them.

Victims who disclose years after being abused or assaulted are now being referred to various services. Counselling services of all kinds feel that the earlier the intervention after the assault the greater the likelihood that the long term effects of the trauma will be minimised but it is also clear that many people who were abused years before have gained considerable help from counselling and psychotherapy years afterwards. They often feel relieved at being able to talk about what happened to them and unburden themselves of guilt, anger and shame.

Male Victims

Rape and serious sexual assault are not committed only against females. The following is an example of a homosexual assault.

George was coming home from a late-night party one winter's evening when he was eighteen. It was about 3 am so there were no buses and he could not get a taxi. He walked along the main road in a city area and he knew that it would take him about forty-five minutes to get home. A car pulled up beside him. He recognised the driver as someone he had met at the party, a man of about thirty whom George remembered him as having been friendly earlier in the evening. This man offered to take George part of the way home as he lived in the same direction. George saw nothing odd in that and he accepted. As they drove they started taking about different things and it was clear they both had an interest in music. The older man suggested that they call by his flat for a drink, rather that going straight to George's house. George agreed, again seeing nothing out of the ordinary in the invitation.

In the flat they started drinking whiskey. George was unused to spirits and noticed that the man poured him a large measure. Half an hour later, while they were drinking more whiskey and listening to music, the older man started talking about sexual matters and about being gay. He asked George if he thought him attractive and started to touch him. George got very uncomfortable and said he wanted to go home. At that point the other man, who was of a stocky build, punched George and insisted on sexual contact. The abuse went on for more than an hour and involved forced oral and anal sex. Whenever George resisted he was punched again even more violently. George was heterosexual and this sexual assault was his only homosexual encounter. When he eventually got out of the man's flat he walked home. It took him days to tell his parents about what happened and they went to the police together.

George went through the same suffering as a female rape victim. He was shocked and numbed for days and then became angry and extremely distressed. He felt violated and dirty and no amount of washing relieved this. He became withdrawn and was afraid of going out at night by himself. The issue of his own sexuality started to worry him greatly. Had he given the man some homosexual signal? Was he now homosexual because of the homosexual activity with the man? Did he suffer from HIV or some other sexually transmitted disease?

One year later he was not fully back to normal. He attended a counsellor for several months and found this useful. The counsellor helped him to vent his anger, rage and frustration. She also helped him talk about the assault itself and his worries about his own sexuality.

Homosexual rape can occur in any setting and George's case is a typical example. Gang rapes can also occur and these are just as distressing for men as when the victim is a female. From time to time one comes across homosexual rape and murder, either as a once-off event or as part of the activities of a homosexual serial killer. In such cases sexual sadism can be part of the picture.

HIDDEN VICTIMS

Forgotten victims are people whom we do not readily identify as victims in any traumatic situation, such as a sexual assault. In rape, the young man or woman who is raped usually has parents and other family members who may be seriously affected. The psychological effects of the assault on the victim may well spill over into the rest of the family situation and cause unhappiness for everyone. The sexual abuse of one's own children is a particular nightmare for every parent. The idea of your child being hurt at all causes distress to most parents but your child being raped, violated and maybe traumatised for life is beyond conceiving of for normal people. It is similar in its impact to your child being badly injured, disfigured or even killed. When it happens the parent may be numbed and shocked, as the victim is, to such an extent that they find it very hard to support the child or young adult.

Another hidden victim is the husband or partner of a rape victim. Most husbands try their best to be supportive to their spouse in every way after an assault. They listen to her crying and going over the incident. They try to help her get through the sleepless nights or the terrified waking from another nightmare. The rape victim may completely lose sexual feeling for her partner for many months. She may be totally unable to deal with her normal activities such as work, housework or caring for her children, putting further pressure on her husband. The children are also deprived of their mother's normal care and attention during these times. This may make the woman feel guilty and further add to her unhappiness. Sometimes this kind of stress in a marriage ends in separation and divorce.

Another issue for the husband as the hidden victim is the man's own feelings towards his wife. She feels soiled and dirty and the husband may feel something similar about her and perhaps have no control over this feeling. She may be uninterested in sex for some time after the assault; he may lose interest as well. He may be unable to get thoughts of his wife's assault out of his mind and think constantly about the attacker. The husband may become obsessed with feelings of anger and revenge towards the rapist. These feelings are understandable but they may cause further strain in the relationship and contribute to the break-up of the marriage. Sometimes husbands have a little nagging suspicion that their wives were responsible in part for what happened and if this feeling is not resolved it can fester and cause its own problems between them. All this was unasked for by the couple and is part of the spectrum of victimisation that serious sexual assaults produce. Excessive drinking by the man or the woman is often a result, and this adds to the problems rather that alleviating anything.

COMPLAINTS BY MENTALLY DISORDERED VICTIMS

Sometimes a person who is mentally ill with a disorder such as schizophrenia or depression makes a complaint of sexual abuse or of rape. A mentally handicapped individual or someone in the early stages of dementia may need to make a similar complaint. What frequently happens is that the police or the prosecuting agency in the jurisdiction decides that such a person should be regarded as unsafe or unreliable as a complainant so the case does not proceed to a criminal prosecution. The legal thinking is that if a conviction were to come about on the basis of the complaint or evidence of such an unreliable witness a great wrong could take place. If there is a lot of physical evidence to back up the complaint the case may be allowed to proceed but there is often a lack of physical evidence in sexual abuse cases, especially if the assault took place more that a few days previously. This seems to suggest that the mentally disordered person has fewer rights than the normal person in terms of making complaints of assault or other victimisation. In many cases, especially in relation to the mentally handicapped, the victim is dependent on a parent or another relative to do the complaining for them.

What of the person who is so seriously mentally ill that they cannot communicate? Likewise, the mentally handicapped person who is unable to understand that he or she has been abused and even if they did, is unable to communicate this information. The same problem exists in the case of some brain damaged individuals and those with advanced dementia. There is at present no real answer to these difficulties, similar to those that exist in the case of young children who have been abused. A small child may not understand that he or she has been abused, and even if they want to tell someone about something nasty that happened to them, they may not have the ability to communicate. Even if the older child is able to communicate effectively they may be considered an unreliable or unsafe witness because of their age. Sometimes the worst abusers walk free because the main witnesses against them are not regarded as reliable or legally safe.

The Victim and the Court

It would be reasonable to expect that the criminal justice system, including the courts, would make special provision for victims in general and victims of sexual assault in particular but this is not the case. Most sexual assault and rape victims say that the investigation of the case, the lead-up to the trial and the trial itself are all extremely traumatising. They often feel that *they* are on trial in some way and find the examination and the cross-examination in a public courtroom very distressing. The issue of whether the acts were consensual is nearly always raised if the case goes to full hearing.

A proportion of offenders plead guilty at the beginning of the trial, which is usually a great relief to the victim. In Ireland, courts must acknowledge a guilty plea in sexual offence cases at the time of sentencing, so this means a judge is unable to impose the maximum allowable sentence in a case even if he wanted to for reasons of public safety. This was established in a supreme court decision which is binding on all courts. Many people, including judges and politicians, are unhappy with this situation.

Many people also feel that the criminal justice system and the courts are excessively concerned with the rights of the offender and not concerned enough with the rights of the victim. The victim is treated on a par with other prosecution witnesses and allowed only minimal expenses, such as travel and subsistence allowances, at the time of the court hearing. There is no effective state compensation system for victims of crime, including sexual crime. Many members of the public and representatives of interested voluntary organisations strongly feel that rape victims should be legally represented at the trial but this has not been fully endorsed by politicians or the court system itself.

An interesting innovation in terms of the rights of the victims of sexual assault and rape is the victim impact report. This concept was originally developed in New

Zealand and adopted in Ireland in the early 1990s. When a defendant is convicted of a sexual crime the court is entitled to seek a victim impact report before sentence is decided on. This is to help the judge to make a decision about the impact of the crime on the individual who was assaulted and to give that person a voice in the proceedings. It usually involves a written report on the victim which is presented to the court but judges normally invite the victim and sometimes a relative, such as a mother, to give oral evidence at this sentencing stage, if they wish to. The question of who is qualified to prepare such a report has been debated from time to time; it is usually a probation officer, psychiatrist, psychologist or social worker. Formerly, reports were prepared by a garda but this is less common now.

When the victim impact report system was adopted it was hailed as being very forward-thinking and useful for the often forgotten victim who had hitherto had no voice in the proceedings. After several years in operation some flaws are emerging. If the victim does very well after an attack and recovers quickly, does that mean that an offender is more likely to get a shorter sentence? Is there subtle pressure on the victim to remain unwell for longer in order the impress the judge? Is there a temptation on the part of the victim to exaggerate her problems in order to get back at the attacker? If any of these suggestions are true, the victim impact report is putting additional and unacceptable pressure on the victim. It may also be unfair to the accused. Should an offender receive a shorter sentence because his victim was psychologically resilient and got better quickly? Should he get a longer sentence because his victim is less able and did not make a good recovery? Should the sentence for similar offences be similar, irrespective of the recovery rate of the victim?

Another issue is that historically society has relieved the victim in criminal cases of the burden of prosecuting the person who offended against them and of being involved in decisions about sentencing. That is why prosecutions are always regarded as matters for the state as opposed to the individual, unlike civil cases. Criminal cases are always identified as the State v Joe Bloggs. We are often uneasy when we hear of the involvement of victims or victims' families in criminal proceedings in other, mostly Muslim, jurisdictions. The victim impact report may unintentionally be allowing a little of that to slip into our legal system. Would victims not be better served by a proper system of compensation? The prosecuting, convicting and sentencing of offenders is a matter for the state and it is really hard to see what benefit all this is to the victim. If the victim gives good evidence in the trial and in the victim impact report, the offender may get a very long sentence. Society in general may be happy with this but it may add more to the victim's burden in terms of guilt. Compensation may be a more positive gesture from a society which claims to be concerned for victims of crime.

What Can Be Done for Victims?

It is important that victims are responded to in a supportive and understanding way by all the agencies that come in contact with them. This is particularly important in the case of victims of sexual crime because they are often completely shattered and damaged by the experience. Police and investigating personnel need to be chosen carefully and trained to deal with these people because it is unacceptable if the victim is further traumatised. In the past some police officers felt that their primary role was the investigation of crime and the apprehension of offenders. The support of the victim is now recognised as being an integral part of the same process. I often hear from victims that they would never have been able to survive the ordeal of the investigation, the months of waiting and the trial itself without the support and care of particular police officers.

If it is felt that the victim is unable to protect or look after themselves, as in the case of children, the mentally handicapped and the elderly or infirm, he or she needs to be protected by the services. This may mean removing the individual to some place of safety such as a hospital or other accommodation to separate them from the alleged abuser. Once the victim is protected the case can be investigated by the agencies involved.

Most rape victims we know about do make good recoveries but a number remain psychologically disabled. Others recover to a great extent but still have residual problems. Nobody knows what happens to the victims who never present to the agencies for help and we can only speculate about how they cope in the long term.

7
VICTIMS OF CHILD SEXUAL ABUSE

'YOU LIKE THIS, MARY, DON'T YOU?'
Mary was very unhappy with how things in her life were turning out. She was in her early thirties, single and living in her own flat. She enjoyed her job as a cook and she liked her present boyfriend. A year prior to being referred to her psychiatric service she had an accident at work. One night in the restaurant she had a bad fall and hurt her back. The injury caused her a lot of distress because she had constant pain and stiffness over several months and could not lift things as before. She often had to take days off sick, which was very unusual for her. Her sleep was disturbed and she became quite irritable with work-mates and others.

Even after the pain and stiffness started to settle Mary's mood continued to be very gloomy. Her relationships with her family and workmates deteriorated and there were many rows.

When she was given an opportunity to talk, Mary described her childhood. Her memory of most of her childhood was patchy. It was really a blank period in her consciousness. She knew she had been abused by her father but never thought about it. She had hardly any memories of her childhood that were not unhappy ones but she had almost completely forgotten or suppressed it. She met her parents about once a month but would not have felt very close to them. The abuse was never mentioned but she had always been sure that her mother knew about it but had been afraid to do anything to protect her daughter.

Soon after the accident at work the abuse returned to haunt her mind. During the day she remembered her father's abuse. Everyone else in the house would be asleep. She slept in a room with her younger sister. She remembered the sound of him taking his trousers off and then pulling the bedclothes back. He told her to be quiet, that it was their 'little secret', or she would be sorry. The abuse happened most weekends and as time went on he told her to be quiet and say nothing or daddy would go to prison. Sometimes he said: 'Bad little girls like you are taken away if they say anything.' She loved her mammy and daddy and she did not want daddy to go to prison nor did she want to be sent away herself. 'You like this Mary, don't you,' he often said. She liked attention from her daddy so she felt guilty and ashamed because she believed she was to blame. That feeling remained with her throughout her life.

Growing up, Mary had put the abuse behind her. It was as if she parcelled it all up neatly and put it into some back room in her mind, never to be looked at again. It was a dark and savage part of her life's experience which was never to re-emerge. She had not really forgotten because she knew of its existence but she erected a barrier which kept it out.

Mary's accident at work traumatised her both physically and psychologically. Her reaction to it was what is seen frequently after bad accidents such as car crashes. She had pain, limitation of movement and felt frustration because of this. She was constantly reminded of the accident and started to feel angry that this should have happened to her. Her mood was a little down, she was weepy for no particular reason and her sleep was disturbed. She was irritable with her family and other people in her environment. These are all typical symptoms in the post-accident person and they tend to settle down in weeks or months after the event.

In Mary's case the accident caused her normal psychological defences to be weakened. For the average person this does not cause any long-term problem because they recover and things return to normal. But the very unpleasant memories of Mary's childhood abuse surfaced and refused to go back into the cocoon in which she enclosed them many years previously. These feelings connected to the sexual abuse by her father had never been dealt with or resolved. Counselling by experts in dealing with sexual abuse victims can help individuals such as Mary. The earlier the psychotherapeutic and counselling input the better.

The Child Victim Presenting to the Services

When a sexual abuse victim presents to the services in childhood it is usually after the case has been disclosed and the community care team is involved. This team is similar throughout Ireland and the UK and includes doctors, social workers and other professionals. Their main goal is to protect children from further abuse, to arrange for treatment and counselling for the victim and to support the mother or other family members as appropriate. By then the police are usually involved.

The effects of sexual abuse tend to be worse if the

abuser is a close relative of the victim. The abuse perpetrated by fathers is usually the most traumatic for the child and the effects of such abuse are likely to be the most long lasting. Betrayal of trust is an important issue for all those who are abused by people they know and this is especially important within one's own family.

It is easy for someone from outside the situation to say that of course the child must report the wrongdoing but for the victim it is not so simple. The abusing father is the only father they have and they may love the father in other ways. Abusers, like other people, often have many sides to their personalities. Sometimes victims say that although they hated what was going on they liked the time alone with the abusing person as it made them feel important in some way. This is a feeling that profoundly confuses the child and may later make them feel guilty as if they were in some way to blame.

The abusing brother can produce the same trauma for the brother or sister victim. The common situation is the older brother abusing the younger sister. The victim may love the older brother quite a lot, admire and look up to him, which means that the victim may like the special attention being paid to her by the hero sibling. They hate the sexual advances and the pain but some part of them enjoys the closeness and the attention. This can be difficult for the child to make sense of and can add to feelings of guilt. Sometimes this type of sibling abuse can go on over many years, even into the late teens and early twenties. The abuse may never be disclosed or may be disclosed only years later when the female victim is married and has children of her own. The psychological effects of the abuse may not fully emerge until then. The victim may realise that the abuser could abuse other children inside or outside the family. He may have children of his own by then and she may fear for their safety.

The grandfather is another possible perpetrator who is difficult to conceive of for the normal person. Sometimes grandfathers abuse their grandchildren as badly as the worst abuser. This can mean fondling or sexual intercourse and can vary in frequency from every few months to daily. The child in this situation has to live through a continuous and brutal nightmare with no hope of escape.

Abuse by mothers is a topic that is not well documented. There are worrying accounts that one comes across from time to time about mothers abusing their children but these hardly ever go as far as the courts.

Over the past few years in Ireland, victims have come forward to report earlier abuse because they saw so much coverage of child sexual abuse in the media. Quite a number say that the reporting of cases in the media revived their own memories of childhood abuse in their own families or in other settings or institutions. These very unhappy memories would not go away for them and so they had to come forward. Others realised only when they had children of their own that the abusers who abused them could go on indefinitely abusing other children. There is sometimes a simplistic feeling among victims that the abuser stopped abusing for good as soon as their own abuse stopped. This is usually far from the truth but sometimes the victim sees this only with the maturity of adulthood and parenthood.

Some children spend some time, months or years, in an institutional setting such as a boarding school or in the care of a local authority. In this situation there is no escape from an abuser and often no one to turn to. The abuse may occur every night and no one will hear your screams. Such children often report their dread of night and darkness. Even when they reach adulthood they can hear the footsteps of their tormentor and the call to follow them. Such children are often so frightened that they believe that all the staff in such institutions are the same so they trust on one. None of the children talk to one another about their experiences and it is only by chance, years later, that they find out that there were many others who had the same experiences. This is something one also sees in family situations where multiple children have been abused. Years afterwards individuals disclose their own abuse only to discover that other sisters or brothers were also being abused.

There are many possible symptoms with which child victims of sexual abuse can present to professionals such as doctors, child psychiatrists, psychologists or social workers. Some obvious medical presentations are pregnancy, venereal disease or physical injury in the genital area but these may not be present in the majority of cases. Many psychological symptoms are non-specific but, taken in the context of complaints of abuse, make a lot of sense. These include nervousness, depressed mood and anxiety. Some children, especially younger children, may regress in their development, may, for example, start bedwetting, having been dry for a long time. Some express a great fear of being away from their mother or from home and others may refuse to go to school. The child's self-esteem is often seriously affected and their academic performance at school usually deteriorates while they become increasingly introverted. The quiet introverted child is frequently a target for the predatory paedophile in the first place. He gives this child special attention and time as he weaves his web of manipulation and abuse around him or her.

Abused children, like abused adults, become very fearful and distrustful of people. They feel alone and abandoned, as if in a nightmare. A child cannot see that this dreadful situation can come to an end and they very seldom realise that they may be able to stop the abuse themselves or arrange to have it stopped by others. Some children develop understandable feelings of anger and hatred toward the abuser and sometimes towards men in general. Others have similar feelings towards their mothers because in their eyes they failed to protect them. Children who were abused in institutions feel this anger towards the people in charge, often a religious congregation. Others feel it towards society in general, a society that put them into care in an institution or foster home but failed to protect them while they were in care.

As a first priority, the child victim of sexual abuse needs to be protected from further abuse and separated from the abuser, whether he is the father, brother, teacher or someone else. Other children must also be protected from the perpetrator. The victim then needs to be given the opportunity to vent frustration and feelings of anger and hatred. He or she must be helped to understand that the abuse was not their fault and that they were not to blame. Some victims go through their whole lives believing that they are responsible for what happened, that it was they who started it all off and that they probably deserved it anyway. They need to be helped to start relating to themselves as individuals again, with rights over themselves and their bodies. Many victims mentally cut off from their bodies and go through the abuse as if it were someone else undergoing the torture.

This process of recovery can take many months or even longer. Many children never recover totally and the majority are probably never given the opportunity to get help. Victims themselves often feel that they do not deserve to be helped. They may feel that there was something bad or unworthy about them in the first place in order for this abuse to have happened to them. Some victims believe throughout a childhood of abuse that sexual abuse is normal and that all children go through it.

In the case of childhood abuse, other family members are very important in the process of recovery. Frequently the mother in an abuse situation needs a lot of help and support. She may have also been abused if it is a case of abuse within a family setting. Both parents would be involved in the therapy process if the abuse occurred outside the family, if the perpetrator was, say, an uncle or some other person in the family's social circle. The relationships within the extended family can sometimes become strained if one family takes the side of the abuser and one the side of the abused.

THE ADULT PRESENTING FOR HELP

The young man, Jim, was twenty-five years old when he presented for help. Since childhood he had kept his abuse secret. He also kept secret his fear that he might be gay or that there might be something wrong with his sexuality. Worries about his sexuality eventually brought Jim to his doctor for help. As a member of a youth club from the age of about twelve he knew a young man, in his late twenties, who was one of the staff at the club. This young man was popular with the children and young teenagers. Jim had friends but was a little unhappy at home because his parents used to fight. He often felt lonely. The youth worker was someone he looked up to, as did the other children. This young man started taking Jim to the cinema, occasionally with other boys but usually by himself. They would go back to the young man's rented house to watch television. After a time, the man started to rub Jim's leg and this developed in to further rubbing and eventually sexual fondling. The abuse went on over three years. Jim enjoyed the attention and the young man persuaded him that this was their special relationship and secret. He made Jim swear to secrecy and this prevented him from disclosing over the years. The child believed that it would be a sin to tell.

When Jim presented it was obvious that he was still under the spell of the young man, even though the abuse had occurred approximately ten years previously. He still felt it was wrong in some way to disclose what went on between them. He had enjoyed the closeness and the attention and as a result he felt as if he was responsible for what had gone on. It took some time to get Jim to understand that what had gone on was the sexual abuse of a child by an adult. Jim feared that he might abuse children himself some day because of what had happened. He felt that perhaps he should not have children of his own because of this.

Jim had many personality problems which were related to the abuse. He had low self-esteem, often suffered from self-doubt and lacked confidence. One area that worried him was his relationships with women. He was able to form relationships with women but they lasted no more than a few weeks, even if he liked the woman a lot. He could never get closer to the woman emotionally. He had sex with many of these women but he often worried about being homosexual because he had enjoyed parts of what went on with the youth club worker. Jim was angry with the man who had destroyed many parts of his experience of growing up and now seemed also to be destroying his adult life. This in itself was distressing for him because parts of him still loved the young man who had given him attention and affection.

It is extremely difficult for any victim to come forward and seek help in sexual abuse cases or to report the abuse. For boys or men it seems to be especially difficult. They often fear that they are homosexual and that if they report what happened everyone will know about their sexuality. Many males who were sexually abused fear that they are at risk of becoming abusers themselves and so decide to stay quiet about it all for fear of being accused of something. They are no more at risk of becoming abusers than any other person in society.

Women who have been victims of abuse have the same difficulties in relationships as men do. They find it hard to trust people, men in particular. Frequently they have problems with emotional closeness and also with intimacy and sexuality. Sexual activity may bring back memories of the original abuse or they may feel very uncomfortable with sex but not know the reason why. Their problems may be a low sex drive, little interest in sex, fear of physical intimacy, difficulties with orgasm or vaginismus. Sometimes one comes across children and young women who have reacted to abuse by becoming over-sexualised. It is as if they try to compensate for the abuse by seeking some kind of comfort in having multiple sexual partners with little feeling for the relationships involved. This can lead to further abuse of a child and unwanted pregnancies, venereal disease and even prostitution in the adult.

A proportion of people who are abused in childhood develop depressive illnesses in later life, which may include the symptoms of low mood, crying, sleep disturbance, loss of interest, loss of appetite and feelings of hopelessness. The memories of the abuse can endlessly preoccupy the thoughts of such an abused person. Some people become suicidal as a result of the abuse and subsequent depression.

Anorexia nervosa is a very serious eating disorder. It typically involves a young woman, usually in her teens, controlling her food intake in an extreme way and losing considerable amounts of weight. The girl's periods usually stop. She may over-exercise and induce vomiting to lose more weight. Anorexia is very difficult to treat and can be chronic. There is a history of childhood sexual abuse in a proportion of anorectics but it is difficult to know what part such abuse plays in the development of eating disorder. This is also the case in people who suffer from bulimia nervosa, another eating disorder which involves indulging in binges of overeating followed by self-induced vomiting. Bulimics tend to maintain their weight but have many difficulties in their lives and personalities.

Some victims, both men and women, have extreme difficulties in their personalities and lead very unhappy lives. A proportion become involved in crime and never relate their problems back to their histories of abuse. Prostitution is a path that both male and female victims may take, as is drug addiction. It is difficult to attribute these ways of life directly to childhood abuse but it is clear that where abuse is part of the life experience of the individual, it plays an important part in subsequent personality development.

Sometimes one comes across such adult victims or alleged adult victims of childhood abuse in the context of prison or when they are charged with various crimes before the courts. The expert advising the court has to disentangle truth from fiction and lies from fantasy in the stories of some accused people. Defendants commonly claim to have been sexually abused because they feel it may be helpful to them in court.

Sometimes when an accusation of child sexual abuse is made, the defence can be that the accuser is unreliable as a witness. This may be because of drug addiction, alcoholism or various personality problems. The person may also have a history of depression or suicidal behaviour. It is very sad that the long-term consequences of the original sexual abuse are sometimes used against the victim to discredit their accounts of the abuse. It is a second abuse of the person.

Most people who have been abused as children never become psychiatric cases and never come forward for help. A proportion develop various psychiatric disorders such as depression and some become suicidal. Some lucky ones seem to put the whole nasty part of their lives behind them and function as normal people. Perhaps they never reach their full potential but there is no way of knowing that. Others have more subtle problems, are quiet, lacking in confidence or never really fitting in. It is as if they have never reached anything near their real potential. But they are hidden victims whose stories are seldom told.

Early psychotherapy and counselling seem to be the best hope for many. In the process of counselling, victims are allowed to vent feelings of frustration, anger and unhappiness. They are helped to piece their lives together again and to approach the future with more hope and optimism. Some need to understand why they behave in certain ways that may cause them unhappiness or why they may relate to others in a destructive or unproductive way. They usually need help with their self-esteem and confidence. Some need help with depressive or suicidal feelings. Others need specific inputs concerning their drug or alcohol problems.

Child sexual abuse has always been with us so it is hard to believe it is possible to eradicate it completely. Education initiatives at primary and secondary school seem to be a useful approach. There is also a small number of programmes internationally that focus on sexual offenders. These are usually group therapy oriented and they try to educate the sexual offender about his own sexuality, the offending behaviour and about the effects of the offending on victims. These programmes, both inside and outside prisons, have the main aim of reducing re-offending among known offenders.

8
Victims of Non-Sexual Crime

Even though there has been a great deal of emphasis over the past decade on the victims of abuse, sexual crime is quite rare compared to other classes of crime such as property offences, including burglaries and shoplifting. Crimes such as burglaries are sometimes thought of as being less important than homicides or rapes but for the people involved they may be very serious indeed. They are reported in annual statistics as either increasing or decreasing from year to year. The newspapers tend not to report them at all. Each statistic represents a very unpleasant experience for some individual or family.

Intruders and the Elderly

Paddy was a seventy-year-old farmer who lived on his own on his small farm. His brother had died several years before. Paddy and his brother were unmarried and they had lived all their lives in the same house on the small-holding. The only other surviving family member was a younger married brother who lived in the city. One evening around 6 pm, Paddy arrived home from the local town. He had done some shopping there and had a pint of beer with some friends. He parked the old Ford outside the cottage. As he bent into the car to get his shopping he was knocked to the ground. He felt a hard bang on the back of his head and hit the side of his head on the car door as he fell.

He was dazed and confused for a few moments. When

he came to, two young men were kicking him as he lay on the ground. 'Where is the money?' they shouted. Paddy was so frightened he did not answer at first, then he mumbled that he had some money in the house. They dragged him indoors and tied him to a chair. Both attackers had masks on, which made them frightening to the old man. They kept shouting about the money and said that they were going to kill him and burn down the house. He told them where his money was. They got £200 in the wardrobe and then ransacked the house. Everything was pulled asunder. When they were finished they beat Paddy again and demanded to know where the real money was. He said he had no more. One of them put a plastic bag over Paddy's head and said he was going to die. He took it off several minutes later as Paddy gasped for air. Paddy was sure they were going to kill him. The attack stopped after about half an hour and the intruders left but they said they would be back. The old man was found by a neighbour several hours later.

The police were called and Paddy later made a statement about the assault. He was taken to the local hospital where he was kept overnight. The elderly man was very shocked and shaken by the experience and needed sedatives that night and for several days afterwards. His wounds needed dressings and one cut on his head received several stitches.

When he moved back into his own house Paddy was unable to settle or to sleep. He had always been a relaxed person but he now became very tense and worried. Every little noise inside or outside the house made him think the intruders were coming back. When he tried to sleep at night he would be haunted by memories of the shouting or images of the masks. If he did manage to get to sleep he often woke up with the terrifying nightmare of having the plastic bag over his head. When this happened his heart would be pounding and he would be sweating and shaking. Sometimes the nightmare seemed worse than the original incident.

Six months later Paddy had improved only a little. He was afraid to go outside the house, especially at night. He tended to stay in bed a lot and he started to neglect his appearance. He took less interest in the farm and in his surroundings. The neighbours were very supportive and one of them made sure to call every day. Before the attack he looked after himself and did his own cooking. He had always been very independent. Now his neighbours had to make sure he took at least one meal every day. They could see that he had no interest in food or anything else, even sport, even though he has always been a football enthusiast. People were saying that he would be better off in a nursing home. Paddy tended to agree with them and his local doctor started to make enquiries for him.

In this incident an elderly but capable and independent person was brutally attacked and robbed. Following the attack he had such a serious post-traumatic stress reaction that he was unable to return to his previous level of functioning. Such victims may have to finish their lives in nursing homes. Others spend weeks or months in hospital because of serious injuries such as fractured bones. Still others have heart attacks or strokes soon after the attack and die, or in the case of a couple, one may die prematurely while the spouse is devastated by the bereavement.

Other elderly victims may seem to recover but their lives are restricted and their ability to cope with day-to-day matters diminished. They may need to see the local doctor frequently, becoming chronic psychiatric patients because of persistent depressive or anxiety symptoms. The attack can alter the victim's whole life.

Victims of Burglaries

Not all victims of burglaries have such a nasty experience as Paddy. In fact most thefts from a person's house involve no contact at all with the offender. The family wake up in the morning and may have finished breakfast by the time they realise that the clock on the mantelpiece is gone and the TV and video recorder missing. Others may return from work or from a few days away to find that the house has been ransacked in their absence. Some burglars are looking for particular items such as video recorders or silver. They may quickly identify what they want and then look at likely places where cash might be, doing minimal damage. Other housebreakers seem to be much more chaotic and destructive. They may empty draws and presses in an almost frenzied fashion and destroy furniture and ornaments.

From time to time one comes across burglaries where the offender leaves his 'calling card'. This is where he defecates or urinates somewhere in the house, for instance on the dining room table. Others destroy decorations and goods with spray paint. Why a burglar has to do these things is anybody's guess but it seems to heighten the thrill or 'buzz' for some offenders. For others it is a disgusting and rude gesture to the inhabitants of the house. Sometimes burglars take bottles of alcohol if they find them in the rooms that they enter. Others drink the alcohol there and the occasional burglar has been found by a startled house-holder in a drunken sleep the next morning.

Many burglars say that they are not deterred by burglar alarms but it seems to be a fact that 80 per cent of burgled houses have no alarms, a percentage so high as to make one doubt the offenders' assertions. One thing they all agree about is the undesirability of a big dog on the premises. Macho offenders will tell you about how easy it is to overcome a dog with a piece of meat but very few burglars will tackle an Alsatian that is protecting his patch.

Even a standard burglary may have a serious effect on the occupants of a house. Friends often ask such people what was taken or how much money they lost. Was there much property damaged? People seldom ask if anyone was assaulted or injured. Assuming no one was hurt, is the property loss the main issue? If the value of the property, the cash or the valuables lost in the incident is high, this may indeed be the most important matter. However, for most people the biggest problem is the fact that their home, their living space, has been invaded. It is compar-able to a woman being sexually assaulted. The people of the house, especially the woman, feel as if the house and in some way the family has been defiled. This feeling is worse if there is a lot of damage to objects or furniture or if the offender actually defiled the place with 'calling cards'. No amount of cleaning seems to remove the dirty feeling. Some people are not satisfied until they change furniture or decorations. Other people find they cannot settle in the house again and move house.

MUGGINGS

The elderly woman was walking into town as usual to do her weekly shopping. She had just collected her pension and also had some extra money that she had saved for the gas bill. All of this was in her purse, which she carried in her handbag. In two weeks time she would be seventy-five. In her bag she also had her travel pass and medical card, her address book and her house keys. There were some items of sentimental value to her such as her own mother's photograph and one of her late husband and her at a dance. She felt lonely when she thought of him. He had died five years previously and she had lived alone since then. Her son and daughter were both married. The daughter visited several times a week with her three small children. They were coming to her that day and she was wondering what they would like for lunch.

As she walked along the familiar street something caught her eye in a shop window and she turned to look. At that point she heard a commotion behind her and the sound of running feet. She was about to turn around when she felt her bag being pulled from her arm. Instinctively she pulled back and she was immediately knocked off balance. First she felt the thud of her knees on the pavement and then punches and tugs from someone behind her. The other assailant yanked the bag off her and in doing so pulled her fully to the ground. She went blank for a few moments and came to, to find that two shop assistants and a passerby had come to her aid. She had hurt her shoulder and banged her head. She was bleeding but she did not seem to notice. All that was in her head was 'They got my pictures.' It took a few minutes more for her to realise that her bag and all its contents, including the money, were gone. When her helpers tried to help her to her feet she was unable to stand. Her legs did not seem to work. All she could think of was what was she going to get for lunch and how was she going to get home?

An ambulance was called and she was taken to the local hospital. She was kept there for most of the day while they determined that she had no broken bones or serious injuries. The head wound needed some stitches and her knee grazes required dressings. At a future point her arm and shoulder injuries may need physiotherapy. The main feature of her presentation in casualty was that she was shocked and badly shaken. During the day she seemed to mumble to herself and cried from time to time. It took the hospital staff several hours to contact her daughter. When she arrived the woman seemed happier and she settled down later on. Her daughter took her home in the evening.

That evening and the next day the police interviewed the victim about what had happened. She went over the story several times. She had not got a good look at her attackers' faces but both had leather jackets. The young man who had pulled her to the ground by pulling the bag had dark hair. The young woman who had pushed and punched her was blonde.

It took the woman several weeks to recover. Her shoulder strain was the slowest to clear up. Sleep continued to be a problem for several months and from time to time she had nightmares about the incident. Now when she shops she always tries to have a friend or her daughter with her. She is nervous on her own downtown. She still loves to have her daughter over to see her, which she does almost every day now. Sometimes she gets irritated with the children but her tolerance is returning to normal. The offenders were never apprehended nor the bag or its contents ever found.

Many people consider a handbag snatch or a mugging a trivial crime but it can have a serious effect on the victim, especially if the assault is particularly violent or the victim is old and frail. From time to time people sustain serious injuries during muggings and handbag snatches. The victim may fall and injure their head or break their arm or hip. Fractures in elderly people may take months to heal and sometimes hip fractures do not mend. Many elderly people are frightened to go out shopping or walking on their own for many months after such an attack, so their lives are greatly restricted by these offenders. Assailants may have forgotten about the snatch in minutes and may have gone on to the next victim with no feelings of guilt or remorse.

In many areas there are victim support services but these are not always easy to locate. The person's own family doctor is usually best placed to know about locally based services such as counselling, psychiatric, psychological and social work agencies. The family doctor may or may not be all that a victim needs. When victims are referred to victim support agencies it is often found that they do not want to attend or else they start attending and then stop. They may resist being viewed as 'patients' who need help and as a result deprive themselves of beneficial support. However, I can understand this resistance on the part of such victims to take on anything resembling a patient's role. A supportive family is very important as this is the main source of help and recovery.

Child Battering

Repeated physical assaults in a domestic situation are usually referred to as child battering or wife battering. Sometimes people have referred to the 'child battering syndrome' and I recall one offender in prison telling me, 'I need special help, doc, because I've got "child battering syndrome".' Derek wore his 'disease' as a badge of distinction and used it as an explanation for his behaviour as if he had no control over it. He was serving a prison sentence for repeatedly beating his three-year-old stepson. 'The child would not stop crying,' he said.

Derek had been living with his common law wife for over two years. She was nineteen and he was twenty. The child was from a previous relationship. She had left home soon after his birth and had had very little contact with her family since. Derek was from a different town and he too had very little contact with his family. They were both unemployed and lived in a council flat. Sandra was six months pregnant.

Their relationship was rocky and they often argued. They both drank a lot of the available cash and they tended to neglect things like the upkeep of their home. When they argued there often was violence between them, not serious violence but both gave as good as he or they got, mostly throwing things or occasionally pushing or slapping each other. They were both very immature.

Derek was sometimes a little jealous of the child.

Sandra loved her son and never neglected him. She spent a lot of time tending to his needs during the day and liked playing with him and reading to him. Derek took care of his stepson whenever Sandra went out with her friends, about once a week. During these times he would become very irritated and intolerant of the child. He often shouted at him to stop crying and this made the situation worse. On numerous occasions he slapped and punched him. Once he twisted the child's arm so that he had to be taken to hospital with a suspected fracture.

One evening when Sandra came home after being out with friends she found Derek standing over the child trying to revive him. He was unconscious and would not wake up. She phoned the ambulance and he was taken to hospital. The child was in intensive care for several days but eventually made a good recovery. The police and social workers were immediately brought in by the hospital authorities. They were very worried for the child's safety because the child had been nearly dead on arrival. They had noticed the bruises and X-rays had shown up healed small fractures to different bones.

Derek admitted repeatedly battering the child 'because he would not stop crying'. Derek was charged with assault and causing grievous bodily harm and was given a prison sentence. Sandra and he never got back together again.

Child battering of this kind is usually perpetrated by males. It may be an immature man in his early twenties who is the child's father or stepfather but any combination of age and relationship is possible. Why do some people, usually men, become violent towards a child in a cruel and sustained way over a long period? There is no satisfactory answer to this question but a common finding is immaturity of personality. The man may feel jealous because of the time the mother spends with the child. He resents this as a child resents his own mother being taken away. This is totally unreasonable when viewed from the perspective of an adult but the batterer can be very egocentric and may view the world as a self-centred child would. Such a person would be very intolerant of the child and the child's needs and as a result hypersensitive to crying. Some battering men may be violent in any case, and also batter their partners. Alcohol may be a complicating factor and the physical abuse may be worse during periods of intoxication.

The abuse itself can be horrific. A child may suffer broken bones and even skull fractures. Brain damage may kill the child or leave him with permanent disability. This may be caused by direct injury to the head or by attempts at strangulation with the hands or by putting a plastic bag over the child's head which cuts off the oxygen supply to the brain. A more recently recognised type of assault that causes brain damage is the perpetrator persistently shaking the child. Shaking can damage the delicate tissues of the brain in the same way that brain damage can occur in professional boxing. Such shaking can also damage tissues such as the retina at the back of the eye and leave the child with impairment of vision or even blindness. Children can also suffer terrible burns from cigarettes or cooker rings or irons.

WIFE BATTERING

The more usual target for battering and physical abuse is the wife or female partner of the male perpetrator. When Miriam and John married they were in their early twenties. They had been going out together for about eighteen months and she was pregnant. He was her first steady boyfriend. Miriam never really felt particularly close to John but she felt that getting married was the right thing to do. Her parents told her she had no option and John's parents felt the same. They lived in a small rural town and what the neighbours thought or said was of major importance. John and Miriam never communicated much. She noticed that he frequently drank to excess but assumed that this was nothing serious. Several months before the wedding he punched her on the arm during an argument. She refused to speak to him for a week but he apologised and she forgave him.

On the day of the wedding John got very drunk. He had to be carried to the taxi and slept through the journey to the hotel. On the first night he started drinking heavily again and stayed away the whole night. The next morning she asked him where he had been and he beat her for more than ten minutes. He said, 'You're mine now and it's none of your business where I've been.'

From then on beatings were commonplace. John would be violent if his dinner was not ready or over some other trivial matter. He beat Miriam many times during the pregnancy and at one point she thought she was going to lose the baby. From the beginning he refused to let her go out with her friends. He also refused to let her visit them or have them visit her. Later he wanted her to stop visiting her own parents. Life became intolerable for her. When the baby was born he was jealous of any time she spent with him.

Later John accused Miriam of having affairs with other men. This was totally untrue but he persisted. He sometimes beat her because of this and during the punches and the kicks he would demand to know the names of the men. Mostly he was drunk during these episodes. He usually hit her in places where the bruises would not be seen, such as her body, shoulders and the tops of her arms or legs. On one occasion she went to the local hospital because she thought her ribs were broken. She told the staff at the hospital that she fallen at home.

After eighteen months of living hell, Miriam left John and returned to her parents' house. He called around repeatedly for the first few weeks and pleaded with her to come home. She refused. Eventually this stopped and he subsequently made an occasional visit to maintain contact with his son.

Luckily Miriam had the strength to escape and stay away. Some women seem unable to do this, perhaps because they are too dependent or too afraid. A number of woman leave and later return because they feel the partner will change. Another small group of battered wives never get the chance to leave because they are killed by their husbands.

Why do some men behave in this way towards their wives or partners? There is no one answer to this question and no satisfactory answer either. Some are immature and self-centred men who bully and abuse the weaker female. A number of them have problems with anger control and can fly off into a rage at very little provocation. Only a small number of these men give into these temper outbursts when they are with other men. They seem to save it all for the woman at home.

In some turbulent and volatile relationships both partners are violent to each other during their arguments. From time to time one comes across cases where the man is the victim of battering. This seems to be much less common than the other way around but it may also be under-reported. It must be very difficult for a man to admit to being battered by his wife or female partner. Such a man would be afraid to look for help, expecting people to ridicule him and not take him seriously. This is a somewhat similar situation to the male who has been sexually abused.

HIDDEN VICTIMS

Robert and Deirdre were married for over twenty years and had two grown-up children. For many years they had been very unhappy as a couple. The children left home as soon as they were able and both were living with their partners. Robert had become increasingly suspicious of Deirdre. He started to believe she was having affairs with different men, something that was completely without foundation. He wanted her to stay at home every night but she could not cope with his increasingly withdrawn way of life and insisted on going out with friends once or twice a week. When she returned home smelling a little of alcohol he would reprimand her and continue his incessant accusations. On several occasions he became violent towards her and this started to worry her. She thought about going to the police but decided to see how things went. One evening when she came home he attacked her verbally and then started beating her. Eventually he strangled her. Twelve months later he was found guilty of murder and sentenced to life imprisonment.

In the above tragic story the mother was the main victim as she lost her life. The father was a victim of his own obsessions and his tendency to rage and violence. He would spend many years in prison and the rest of the family, including his children, made it clear that they wanted nothing more to do with him. The hidden victims are the two grown-up children, their children and the extended family.

The children were torn in different directions psychologically because of what happened. They loved their mother very much and they were devastated by her loss. She was a loving mother and grandmother to their small children. They had loved their father in the past but less so in latter years. They saw him as a difficult person who was stifling their mother. But he was still their father and they found it difficult to cope with the fact that he was a murderer in prison and that the person he had killed and deprived them of was their mother. People in this situation also feel guilty about whether they could have done something to prevent the killing. In this case the children of the dead woman received support from local friends but the neighbours all talked and turned to look if they met them in the local pub. The children wondered if the stigma would remain in their family throughout their lives and the lives of their children. Their concerns about stigma and guilt are similar to those of a family which has lost a loved one through suicide.

When an individual dies, especially a young man or woman, the whole family suffers because of the loss. The spouse and children are usually the worst affected but parents and siblings also suffer. A violent death adds greatly to the suffering of those left behind. In the case of homicide deaths the family of the victim have to cope with thoughts of hatred and even feelings of revenge, such as may have been completely alien to the family up to this. The spouse, children and extended family of the offender are also victims.

Two men in their mid thirties had known each other for many years. They had had a disagreement about money for a few weeks, nothing too serious. On the night in question they were both intoxicated, although neither would have been described as a heavy drinker. The row erupted again and one man took out a knife, which he would sometimes carry because of his work. He stabbed the other man, who died in hospital from a single stab wound to the chest. The assailant was convicted of manslaughter and sentenced to eight years in prison. His wife and four children had to cope with the fact that their husband and father had killed someone. The dead man's family lived quite close by and both families had known each other for years. The children went to the same schools and met each other every day; the spouses met each other frequently on the street or at the shops. The family of the offender had to cope with what he had done and also with the fact that he was in prison, a criminal. Added to this was the anger and resentment they could feel from the other, bereaved family. The incomes of both families were greatly diminished and they found it difficult to cope financially. These victims had to suffer the consequences of the actions of one man, although they had no part at all in what happened.

There are many examples of hidden victims in homicide cases, for instance where a man is killed in the course of a burglary. His wife and children have to cope with the sudden and violent death of the loved one, the financial consequences, and their anger and hatred towards the offender. There is no compensation for them. The offender will eventually be released from prison – that is, if he is apprehended – but there is no release from the life sentence of the bereaved family.

Helping Hidden Victims

Services are available to help many victims, including hidden victims, and the family doctor is best placed to link people with them. Victims often have a need to talk about what happened to them and to express feelings of anger and resentment. Such feelings are usually directed toward the assailants but sometimes also towards a society and a system that seems unconcerned about their plight. Counselling by the family doctor or other agencies such as the psychiatric, psychological and social services can help. Financial compensation would be really helpful for most, because of the financial hardship which is nearly always part of being a victim of whatever kind. Such compensation would also officially recognise what has happened to them. Who should pay for such compensation? The offender if he can afford to; if not, I suppose, the state is the obvious conduit for society's funds.

PART III
PSYCHIATRY AND CRIME

Part III

PSYCHO...

9
FORENSIC PSYCHIATRY

THE MIND OF THE CRIMINAL

The workings of the human mind and the debate about what constitutes normality and what mental illness have always fascinated the public. What is sanity and conversely what does the legal concept of insanity mean? Most people will have an opinion about these issues, not surprisingly, since the majority of households in modern society have had some contact with psychiatric problems in the nuclear or extended family.

The general public is similarly fascinated by the mind of the criminal. The nastier the crimes the greater the public interest, for example the crimes committed in Gloucester by Fred and Rosemary West and recently brought to light. Serial killing, especially where sexual offending in involved, seems to absorb the public imagination endlessly.

The discipline of forensic psychiatry combines crime and psychiatry, two of the most interesting fields of human knowledge and debate. It is a specialised area within psychiatry in which the psychiatrist's role is to examine, assess and treat the mentally disordered offender. In the course of such a job the forensic psychiatrist meets many offenders, both 'normal' and 'abnormal'. He or she works in many settings such as prisons and courts and in both security and ordinary psychiatric hospitals. Forensic psychiatrists deal with the whole range of psychiatric disorders in these settings but their patients will nearly always have committed an offence or be charged with an offence as well as needing the help of a psychiatrist. To understand the role of a forensic psychiatrist and the connection between crime and mental disorder, one must know a little both about psychiatry and about crime and the criminal justice system.

Medicine is broken up into different specialities such as general surgery, paediatrics, general practice and pathology, specialities that seem constantly to increase in number. Psychiatry deals with mental illness and mental disorder. Of course, all the clinical specialities deal with some psychiatric problems, in particular general practitioners or family doctors, but these types of problems are the main work of the psychiatrist.

The training of a psychiatrist is similar to that of any other medical specialist in that he or she must qualify in medicine and complete an intern year. The doctor then starts working as a junior psychiatrist and gains experience and knowledge by study and by working in different jobs. He or she has to pass a very challenging postgraduate examination around the third or fourth year of training. Over about seven or eight years the person progresses from being a senior house officer to a registrar and then a senior registrar, the final goal being an appointment as a consultant psychiatrist. In Ireland we have about twelve hundred medical consultants; of these two hundred are consultant psychiatrists.

Psychiatry is itself broken up into speciality areas: general adult psychiatry, child psychiatry, old age psychiatry, the psychiatry of mental handicap. A small number of psychiatrists specialise in psychotherapy, some practising as psychoanalysts.

Forensic psychiatry, also called legal psychiatry, is another such speciality. Of the two hundred consultant psychiatrists in Ireland, two are forensic psychiatrists. In the UK they are slightly more numerous but still a rare breed. The term 'forensic' in the context of psychiatry means the court. The word comes from the Latin *forum*, which was where the Romans held courts of law.

Forensic psychiatrists are not, as the public sometimes assumes, involved in the investigation of crime or the conviction of defendants as forensic scientists are. Forensic scientists may have to analyse samples of blood or other materials such as hairs or fibres or match fingerprints or DNA samples. Forensic scientists nearly always work for the prosecution in criminal cases. Forensic psychiatrists may work on the side of the prosecution or the defence or sometimes act for the court itself.

The role of the forensic psychiatrist is to assess and treat the mentally abnormal offender in prison or in a hospital setting, which may be an ordinary psychiatric hospital or a special security facility. Many forensic psychiatric patients are also assessed and treated as outpatients. In prison the psychiatrist tries to identify prisoners who may become mentally ill or are suicidal and may transfer them to a psychiatric hospital for treatment. Forensic psychiatrists have other specific psychiatric functions in the criminal justice process.

To summarise briefly, among the most common psychiatric disorders from which criminals as well as non-criminals suffer are:

- *schizophrenia*, which may affect about 1 per cent of the population and may involve auditory hallucinations, delusions, thought disorder, behavioural disturbance. The treatment involves the use of antipsychotic medications, either by tablet or long-acting injections and a mixture of other therapy such as family work, psychotherapy and occupational therapy.
- *manic depression*, primarily a mood disorder, a common form of which is clinical depression. The opposite mood disorder is mania, which is a 'high'. The stereotype of the manic-depressive patient is one who experiences episodes of depression and episodes of mania at different times. Various medication and therapies are used, such as lithium for manic depressives.
- *alcoholism*, which is so widespread that it is often overlooked. It is one of the greatest contributors to crime. Alcohol abuse and intoxication are firmly associated with domestic violence, homicide and all types of sexual offences from incest to rape. Drunken drivers leave countless dead bodies behind them on the roads and even larger numbers of victims who are relatives of those deceased. Many psychiatrists no longer consider alcoholism a medical or psychiatric matter but some centres still specialise in alcohol problems.
- *drug addiction*, especially heroin abuse, which is an extremely important issue in crime and is related to the international rise in serious crimes of violence. Many heroin addicts need £200 a day to feed their habit and will acquire that money by criminal means if necessary.

- other psychiatric disorders such as *severe anxiety and tension*, *phobias* such as *agoraphobia, panic attacks* and *claustrophobia* and *social phobia*, eating disorders like *anorexia nervosa* and *bulimia*.
- *personality disorders*, which are controversial in that some people believe that they are not really part of the responsibility of psychiatry.

The most extreme example of a person with such a disorder is the *sociopath* – someone with an antisocial personality disorder. Some sociopaths are loners while others are superficially gregarious, but all are intensely self-centred. A proportion are addicted to alcohol or drugs and some may have a history of attempted suicide from overdoses or wrist slashing. Sociopaths may become involved in crime, including violent crime, and a striking feature is their total lack of remorse or concern for the victim. *Psychopath* is a term formerly used for the sociopath; an even older description is *moral insanity*. This term captures some of the important elements of the problem. The individual in question may present as pleasant and reasonable but they have absolutely no feelings for other people as human beings. They are simply there to be exploited. The ruthless hit-man may be a sociopath. In cold blood and without remorse he kills people for money. There are many lesser examples of this problem in the habitually violent offenders who kill, injure or sexually assault people with no concern for the victims as people.

In the 1960s there was greater acceptance of the concept of sociopath and serious personality disorder and psychiatrists were thus interested in trying to treat or manage these individuals. Courts in the UK, for instance, were more likely to order the detention of offenders with 'psychopathic disorder' in institutions like Broadmoor if they had committed serious offences such as homicide. They were managed by means of a therapeutic environment and detention over a number of years. A proportion of those termed 'sociopaths' or 'psychopaths' tend to become less difficult and disruptive as they get into their mid thirties. Since the mid 1970s the climate of opinion has changed; people are now more inclined to use words and phrases like 'evil' and 'bad not mad' to describe such offenders. As a result they are now more likely to be given a prison sentence than be committed for treatment to a hospital.

PSYCHIATRY IN THE CRIMINAL JUSTICE SYSTEM

If a person is charged with an offence in Ireland, he or she is usually brought before the district court the following morning. In the UK the equivalent court is the magistrates' court. If the offence is minor the court may deal with it there and then; more usually the accused must return the following week. The defendant is remanded on bail or in custody. If the offence is serious, such as a serious assault or a homicide, the defendant is brought back to the same district court every week until the state has gathered all the statements and other evidence together in the form of the book of evidence. The next main function of the district court is to commit the proceedings to the Circuit Court or the Central Criminal Court, which is a division of the High Court. (The equivalent in the UK is the Crown Court.) When the issue is mentioned in the higher court a trial date is fixed. This may be six or nine months away. If the person has been in custody from the initial district court hearing he may be in custody for nearly a year by the time he comes to trial. Such a person is technically not guilty during that time and may well be found not guilty at the trial itself.

The trial process is similar in the different court levels. At the beginning of the process the charges are read out to the person and he is asked to plead guilty or not guilty. If he pleads not guilty a trial takes place in which the prosecution or state team present evidence against the accused and the defence team then presents the person's defence to the charges. In the higher courts this is all done very slowly and the whole story unfolds like a drama with witnesses from either side being questioned by their own side and then cross-examined by the other team. In the district court in Ireland and the magistrates' court in the UK the business is conducted in a more hurried way because of the numbers of cases being handled. Despite this, the lower courts handle more than 90 per cent of all cases of any kind. In the higher courts the cases are usually heard by a judge and jury. The jury determines guilt or innocence and if the verdict is guilty the judge decides on the appropriate sentence. In the lower courts the judge decides on both verdict and sentence.

If the accused is found not guilty he or she may walk free from the court. If he is found guilty the judge may impose a prison sentence, probation or some other penalty such a community service. If a prison sentence is the outcome he is usually taken to a remand prison and may later be sent to a committal prison to serve most of the time.

If the defendant is found guilty of murder the judge must sentence him or her to life imprisonment. This usually means about ten years in prison and the rest of the person's life on 'life licence'. Such a person may have to keep in touch with the local police station or other agency and if there is any recidivism, even a minor offence, the Department of Justice in Ireland or the Home Office in the UK may order the arrest of the person. The minister has discretionary powers about the length of the period of detention. A life sentence does actually mean life and some offenders may never leave prison at all because of the nature of their crimes.

Psychiatry has different roles at different stages of the criminal justice system. A prisoner may become mentally unwell while on remand before conviction or before sentencing or while serving a sentence. Such a person may have a past history of psychiatric illness and may have a diagnosis of schizophrenia or manic depressive disorder. Other prisoners develop a mental disorder for the first time while in prison. They may become acutely distressed because of some problem inside the prison, such as intimidation, or because of something happening outside the prison, for example parents or a loved one becoming very ill or dying. Sometimes a prisoner becomes very unhappy when he realises that his marriage is breaking up and that his wife will leave him or if he believes that his wife is having an affair. Many of these reactions to stress, though serious, are short-lived and the prisoner may recover within a few weeks, particularly if he or she is temporarily transferred to a psychiatric facility such as the Central Mental Hospital. When a prisoner is transferred out of prison for such assessment and treatment it is usually to the unit or facility where the visiting psychiatrist to the prison works. This means that there is continuity of care where possible.

Some prisoners may be acutely suicidal and a proportion try to kill themselves. A number succeed in killing themselves, usually by hanging or drug overdose. Prison suicides, which are widely reported in the media, are very traumatic occurrences both for the families of the dead people and for prison staff.

Drug addicts also cause difficulties for prison staff and for themselves. They may use illicit substances in prison and encourage others to use drugs or even become addicts for the first time. Some offenders go into prisons with no drug problem, only to be released later with a drug problem and a HIV infection. Prisoners with a drug addiction are often very distressed in the early part of their imprisonment because they may be withdrawing from heroin or strong, addictive sedative medications and pain killers. In general they are given a reducing daily dose of the heroin substitute, methadone.

The psychiatrist may be asked to give an opinion to the court, the prosecution or defence teams at different times during the trial process. Before the trial starts he or she may be asked whether or not the defendant is fit to plead. Fitness to plead is related to the person's ability to understand what he is charged with, what pleading means and whether he is able to properly instruct his legal advisers. If this issue is raised it is ultimately decided by a court and if the person is found unfit to plead he is committed to a psychiatric hospital until he is fit to plead. If he is unfit to plead because of depression but this gets better in a couple of months he will be brought back to court. However, if the unfitness is due to mental handicap or an intractable form of schizophrenia the defendant will probably not be fit again, even after a period of treatment. Consequently, in theory, a person could be permanently committed to a psychiatric institution by a court although they have not been found guilty of a crime. This very seldom arises in practice because the courts and the legal teams on both sides try to deal with the situation in the most practical and humane way possible. This may mean having the charges dropped, if they are not too serious, so that the individual can be transferred to his catchment area psychiatric service for care and treatment. If the charges are serious it may not be possible to avoid the issue of fitness.

If a psychiatrist is asked to give evidence in the middle of a trial it is usually on the question of whether the person was responsible for his actions at the time of the alleged offence. In Ireland this involves the insanity defence. The court is interested in knowing if the person was suffering from a 'disease of the mind' at the time. That phrase was coined in 1883 and today it approximates to schizophrenia or a serious depressive illness. Other psychiatric diseases are sometimes allowed as well. It must also be shown that because of this disease of the mind the person did not know what he was doing or they did not know that what he was doing was wrong. The third possibility allowed is that he was unable to stop himself from acting as he did because of this disease.

If a defendant is found guilty but insane he or she is committed to the Central Mental Hospital at the pleasure of the government. We usually have one or two guilty but insane cases in Ireland each year. The vast majority of such cases are in homicide cases. In the UK, in murder cases only, the usual psychiatric defence is 'diminished responsibility'. If it can be shown that the person had 'an abnormality of mind' which 'substantially diminished' his or her mental responsibility at the time of a killing the charge is reduced to manslaughter. This defence is not as restrictive as the guilty but insane defence. The important issue for the defendant in these verdicts is that the judge can give any sentence he or she sees fit, not the mandatory life sentence. However, in approximately one-third of these manslaughter verdicts, the judge still gives a life sentence.

The next stage in which psychiatric evidence is used is in the sentencing phase of the trial. The defendant has been found guilty and the judge is deciding on the appropriate sentence. The defence team will try to bring everything relevant in the offender's background to the notice of the judge, especially information that may not have fully come to light in the trial, such as a past psychiatric history, problems with alcohol or drugs, a positive HIV status or serious family difficulties. It is reasonable to put all of these matters before the court for consideration. Sometimes people label this information 'sob stories' but this is to ignore the fact that offenders are human beings, too, with a history, parents and problems, a family, perhaps a spouse and children. No matter how grievous the offence the court must take all relevant matters into consideration in passing sentence.

CRIME AND PSYCHIATRIC DISORDERS

People often assume that there is a link between mental disorders and crime. There *is* a link but it is a weak one. The association depends on the type of crime and the category of illness or disorder. In about 30 per cent of homicide perpetrators there are serious psychiatric disorders such are alcoholism, depression and schizophrenia. Psychiatric disorder is a broad phrase and includes substance abuse, personality disorders, mental handicap and mental illness. The term 'mental illness' is more restrictive and refers only to the more formal illnesses such as schizophrenia and manic depression.

As regards sexual offenders, such as rapists and child sexual abusers, there is little association; one finds only slightly more mental illness than in the general population. If the victim of a rape is elderly we more frequently find mental illness in the offender. About 60 per cent of rapists and about 50 per cent of incestuous fathers have serious alcohol problems.

There is little association between mental illness and property offences. If there is a problem one sees over and over again in such offenders, who may be burglars and muggers, it is heroin addiction. Addicts may also be HIV positive, which causes its own psychiatric complications. Some offenders who are HIV positive feel they have nothing to lose and no reason to remain out of trouble.

Drug addiction is not an excuse for wrongdoing in our courts and it is certainly not an excuse for the gratuitous violence that one sees more and more inflicted on victims of all ages these days, especially on old people. Neither is voluntary intoxication a defence to crime, nor alcoholism. However, the court may take into account the efforts that person makes to get treatment for their problem and to remain drug or alcohol free. People with drug and alcohol addiction problems deserve all the help society can provide but much depends on the willingness of addicts to recognise their problems and to change.

If we look at the association between crime and mental illness from the mental illness perspective we see a different picture. Schizophrenia is weakly associated with crime: the commonest type of offence committed by such a person is stealing food from a shop because he is hungry. From time to time a person with schizophrenia kills someone because of delusions or hallucinatory voices; such an offence makes a spectacular news stories. (It is regrettable that such stories foster the myth that schizophrenics are dangerous.) Depression is rarely linked with crime, although from time to time a depressed person kills someone, usually a family member and sometimes their own child. Personality disorders, the sociopathic type, are associated with crimes of violence of all kinds from wife battering and sexual offences to murder. Alcohol abuse and alcoholism are associated with all types of violence, especially homicide and sexual offences. Heroin addiction is seen very frequently in property offences and more recently in property offences where violence is perpetrated.